WHY CHRIST CAME

WHY CHRIST CAME

31 Meditations on the Incarnation

Joel R. Beeke
and
William Boekestein

Reformation Heritage Books
Grand Rapids, Michigan

Why Christ Came
© 2013 by Joel Beeke and William Boekestein

Reformation Heritage Books
2965 Leonard Street NE
Grand Rapids, MI 49525
616-977-0889 / Fax 616-285-3246
orders@heritagebooks.org
www.heritagebooks.org

Printed in the United States of America
13 14 15 16 17 18/10 9 8 7 6 5 4 3 2 1

Psalm selections from *The Psalter* (Grand Rapids: Reformation Heritage Books, 1999).

The authors wish to express their appreciation to Rev. Dick Moes for contributing chapters 23 and 24.

Library of Congress Cataloging-in-Publication Data

Beeke, Joel R., 1952-
  Why Christ came : 31 meditations on the incarnation / Joel R. Beeke and William Boekestein.
     pages cm
  ISBN 978-1-60178-268-7 (pbk. : alk. paper) 1. Jesus Christ—Person and offices—Meditations. 2. Incarnation—Meditations. I. Title.
  BT203.B4465 2013
  232'.1—dc23
                                        2013018298

For additional Reformed literature, request a free book list from Reformation Heritage Books at the above regular or e-mail address.

CONTENTS

PREFACE

Traditionally, at Christmastime we think about the story of Christ's birth. It *feels* like Christmas when we picture Joseph and Mary, the shepherds, the angels, and the manger containing the Christ child. But to appreciate the magnitude of the main point of the story—that the eternal Son of God assumed our flesh-and-blood human nature—we need to learn from the rest of the Bible why Christ came to earth.

Sadly, many who vehemently argue the need to "keep Christ in Christmas" can probably say very little about the reality and practical significance of the incarnation. Learning the reasons for Christ's advent will help us more deeply celebrate His birth, allow us to see more clearly how it is connected with the rest of His ministry, and help us understand its importance for our lives. Understanding why Jesus came to earth also has apologetic value. Suppose someone asked you, "Why did Jesus come to earth?" You could probably come up with one or two reasons. As true as those reasons might be, they would only begin to communicate the richness of Christ's incarnation.

"Why" is a marvelous teacher because it helps us identify the meaning of the events we observe. Rudyard Kipling called the interrogative "why" one of the "six honest serving men" who taught him all he knew. Christ Himself frequently employed this "serving man" as He taught about His first coming. Answering the "why" question should also enlarge our vision for the season of Advent and Christmas, helping us answer important questions like, "Why are we gathering as church and family?" "Why do we have special commemorations at this time of year?" "Why does this season bring us hope?"

The psalmist says all creation declares the glory of God (Ps. 19:1). Nothing, however, glorifies God as much as the incarnation of His Son. As Charles Spurgeon exclaimed, "Sing, sing, O universe, till thou hast exhausted thyself, yet thou canst not chant an anthem so sweet as the song of the Incarnation!"[1] John Owen observed, "We can only adore the mysterious nature of it;—'great is this mystery of godliness'" (1 Tim. 3:16).[2]

Likewise, this little book cannot begin to exhaust the riches of the great mystery that God became man. Many more reasons could be given. In addition to the reasons given in this book, Christ came to earth

- to send fire (Luke 12:49–50)
- to redeem us from the law (Gal. 4:4–5)
- to be the Savior of the world (1 John 4:14; John 12:47)
- to be received in the Father's name (John 5:43)
- to give abundant life (John 10:10)
- to reveal the Father (Matt. 11:27; John 14:9)
- to preach deliverance to captives (Luke 4:18)
- to be an example of meekness (Matt. 11:29)
- to fulfill God's promise as the seed of the woman (Gen. 3:15)
- to give us the Holy Spirit (John 7:39)

With John, we can say that if all the reasons for which Christ came were written down, "I suppose that even the world itself could not contain the books that should be written" (John 21:25). The number of reasons for which Christ came into the world may ultimately surpass the number of people He came to save.

We offer these thoughts with the prayer of the apostle Paul: "That Christ may dwell in your hearts by faith; that ye, being rooted and grounded in love, may be able to comprehend with all saints what is the breadth, and length, and depth, and height; and to know the love of Christ, which passeth knowledge, that ye might be filled with all the fulness of God" (Eph. 3:17–19).

Aside from Scripture and biblical commentaries, some other helpful books on the incarnation of Christ include *On the Incarnation of the Word of God* by Athanasius; *Emmanuel, Or, The Incarnation of the Son of God the Foundation of Immutable Truth* by M. F. Sadler; *Christ's Incarnation, the Foundation of Christianity* by Charles Spurgeon; *The Incarnation of Christ* by Edwin H. Gifford and Samuel J. Andrews; *The Virgin Birth of Christ* by J. Gresham Machen; *The Story of the Christ Child* by Leon Morris; *The Person of Christ: A Biblical and Historical Analysis of the Incarnation* by David F. Wells; *The Word Became Flesh: A Contemporary Incarnational Christology* by Millard J. Erickson; *The Christ of Christmas* by James Montgomery Boice; and *Why on Earth Did Jesus Come?* by John Blanchard.

TO DO THE WILL
OF THE FATHER

*For I came down from heaven, not to do mine own will, but
the will of him that sent me.*
                                                    JOHN 6:38

*Then said I, Lo, I come (in the volume of the book it is writ-
ten of me,) to do thy will, O God.*
                        —HEBREWS 10:7; cf. PSALM 40:7–8

Jesus came to earth to do the will of the Father. Ultimately,
the will of God is His righteous decree that determines all
that comes to pass and causes all things to work together
for His glory (Eph. 1:11; cf. Deut. 29:29). Everything that
comes to pass is the will of God, and He accomplishes that
in Christ (Col. 1:16–17). But when Christ speaks about
coming to do God's will, He is referring to the will that
God has revealed "unto us and to our children for ever, that
we may do all the words of this law" (Deut. 29:29). God's
revealed will is breathed out of His heart and establishes His
expectations for His people.

It may surprise us, then, to hear Jesus refer to two wills:
His own and His Father's. In doing so, Jesus opens a win-
dow on His humanity. As Andrew Murray says, "Christ had
a human will. For instance, he ate when he was hungry, and

he shrank from suffering when he saw it coming."[1] While His will was not sinful, Jesus still had to deny it. In taking on flesh, Christ undertook the ultimate challenge of conforming His human will to His Father's divine will.

Jesus met that challenge; He did the will of God in all things. He performed every duty of the law (Matt. 5:17) and resisted all temptation to transgress it. At the end of His earthly life He could say, "I have finished the work which thou gavest me to do" (John 17:4).

James 4:17 says, "To him that knoweth to do good, and doeth it not, to him it is sin." We commit sins of omission every day, but Jesus never did. Indeed, He sometimes went out of His way to heal just one person (Mark 5:1–20). He showed compassion to people who were guilty of notorious sins (John 4:1–30; 8:1–11). The disciples accused their master of being unreasonable when He fed crowds of five thousand and then four thousand, because no one could be expected to provide for such multitudes (Mark 6:35–37). But Jesus had compassion on them (Matt. 15:32). In His entire ministry, Jesus showed that God's servants must not fail to do all that is commanded them (Luke 17:10).

Jesus' obedience to God's will is especially revealed in His fulfillment of the unique task of redeeming and preserving His people according to His Father's eternal plan. He says in John 6:38–40:

> For I came down from heaven, not to do mine own will, but the will of him that sent me. And this is the Father's will which hath sent me, that of all which he hath given me I should lose nothing, but should raise it up again at the last day. And this is the will of him that sent me, that

> every one which seeth the Son, and believeth on him, may
> have everlasting life: and I will raise him up at the last day.

Jesus' obedience was particularly focused on the sheep He came to save. His mother, Mary, sang, "He that is mighty hath done to me great things" (Luke 1:49). As we study Jesus' obedience in the pages of Scripture, we can say, "It was all for us!" (cf. Gal. 2:20).

Not one of the Father's expectations went unfulfilled in Christ. When Christ said, "It is finished," He meant it (John 19:30). By His obedience to God's will, even in the things that He suffered, He secured salvation for us. As our high priest, Christ teaches us that we have no other way of dealing with our moral failure and its penalty than to come to God and say, "Nothing in my hand I bring, / Simply to thy cross I cling."

As we study the early chapters of the Gospels, it is difficult to feel the full weight of Jesus' statement: "I come…to do thy will, O God." But later, especially as we read about Christ in the garden of Gethsemane, we begin to sense the depth of that commitment. In the garden Jesus wrestles with the reality of Isaiah 53:10: "Yet it pleased the LORD to bruise him." In the garden Christ was "exceeding sorrowful, even unto death" and "sore amazed" (Matt. 26:38; Mark 14:33). Paintings of Christ praying while He serenely looks up to heaven greatly distort the reality of His garden experience. In Gethsemane Christ lost His composure, falling to the ground in agonizing prayer (Mark 14:35).[2] The overwhelming terror of bearing God's judgment against our sins pressed out of Him great drops of bloody sweat.[3] Still, Jesus submitted to His Father, praying, "Not what I will, but what thou wilt" (Mark 14:36).

According to John Calvin, Christ's coming to earth to do God's will communicates two things. First, it exalts Christ as the only human who was obedient to God's will. Jesus' life clearly teaches us that we cannot and will not do God's will. That being the case, we need a mediator. The good news of the gospel is that Christ has come to do God's will as the Mediator for those who trust in Him.

Second, Calvin explains, this text "stimulates us all to render prompt obedience to God; for Christ is a pattern of perfect obedience for this end, that all who are His may contend with one another in imitating Him, that they may together respond to the call of God and that their life may exemplify this saying, 'Lo, I come.'"[4]

> The off'ring on the altar burned
> Gives no delight to Thee;
> The hearing ear, the willing heart,
> Thou givest unto me.
>
> Then, O my God, I come, I come,
> Thy purpose to fulfill;
> Thy law is written in my heart,
> 'Tis joy to do Thy will.
>
> — versification of Psalm 40:6–8
> from *The Psalter*, no. 109:1–2

TO SAVE SINNERS

This is a faithful saying, and worthy of all acceptation, that Christ Jesus came into the world to save sinners; of whom I am chief.
— 1 TIMOTHY 1:15

For then must he often have suffered since the foundation of the world: but now once in the end of the world hath he appeared to put away sin by the sacrifice of himself.
— HEBREWS 9:26; cf. 1 JOHN 1:9; 3:5

In Christ's first coming, He implemented a rescue plan conceived in the mind of God before the foundation of the world. He did not come to promote holiday cheer, boost end-of-year sales, or serve as the central figure in a nativity scene. He came to save sinners.

To save sinners, Christ had to put away what makes people sinners—namely, sin. At the dawn of man's history, sin, like an unwelcome virus, infected mankind easily enough. But how could it be exterminated? God was already answering this question through the Old Testament sacrificial system. One of the main themes in the epistle to the Hebrews is the repetitious labors of Old Testament priests: "And they truly were many priests, because they were not suffered to continue by reason of death" (Heb. 7:23). Morning and evening, priests placed burnt offerings for sin on an altar, the fire of which was never to go out (2 Chron. 13:11; Lev. 6:12).

Nonetheless, sins were not fully extinguished through this system (Heb. 10:4). Old Testament sacrifices were merely a shadow, or copy, of what was to come (Heb. 9:23); thus, the priesthood of Aaron could have sacrificed burnt offerings for a million years without putting away a single sin. The writer of Hebrews says the seed of Adam needed a better priesthood to put away sins—a priesthood "after the order of Melchisedec" (Heb. 7:17; cf. Ps. 110:4). Likewise, a better sacrifice offered in a better tabernacle was necessary. When a truly perfect sacrifice was offered in the tabernacle of heaven, sin would finally be put away. Hebrews 9:24–26 says,

> For Christ is not entered into the holy places made with hands, which are the figures of the true; but into heaven itself, now to appear in the presence of God for us: nor yet that he should offer himself often, as the high priest entereth into the holy place every year with blood of others; for then must he often have suffered since the foundation of the world: but now once in the end of the world hath he appeared to put away sin by the sacrifice of himself.

Christ put away the sins of many first by carrying them to the cross, and then to the grave (Heb. 9:28). The sins of God's people were crucified and buried in Christ (Rom. 6:4–5). So fully has Christ purged the believer's sins that Hebrews 9:28 adds, "Unto them that look for him shall he appear the second time without sin unto salvation." How staggering is the thought that we can *eagerly* anticipate the return of the Savior who was wounded for our transgressions!

A man began working for a builder. The first morning, the boss gave clear instructions on how to cut some boards and then left to pick up some materials. After about an hour, the new employee realized that he had cut all of the boards a few inches short. From that point on, he dreaded his boss's return. Like the new employee, sinners don't meet the requirements; Romans 3:23 tells us that "all have sinned, and come short of the glory of God." Believers can thank God, though, that they do not have to anticipate the return of Christ with dread as the new employee did! Redeemed sinners can be so confident that Christ has put away their sin that they can look forward to His return as a day of salvation.

The Scottish divine Samuel Rutherford was on his deathbed when he was summoned to court for refusing to conform to the new forms of worship decreed by the king. Sensing that his death was near, Rutherford said, "I will soon stand before a greater judge, and this one is my friend!"

A minister once sat by the bed of a dying man in a nursing home. As they talked, the man began to recall some of his past sins. He started to weep and then blurted out, "I'm such a terrible, hell-worthy sinner!"

The minister said, "That's wonderful!" Sensing the man's confusion, the minister explained: "You *are* a terrible, hell-worthy sinner. But it is wonderful that you know it, for Christ came to earth for people exactly like you."

Paul doesn't say that he is merely a terrible sinner; he says he is the *worst*. He isn't exaggerating, for he has been guilty of blaspheming Christ, persecuting the church, and injuring innocent people. Those were heinous sins indeed. Yet Paul refuses to focus on the greatness of others' sin to minimize his own. He sees his own sins in the light of God's holy law and perfect character. He also realizes that had he been the only sinner in the world, Christ would still have had to shed every drop of His precious blood to save him.

Great sinners need a great Savior. That is exactly what Christ is, for He is "able also to save them to the uttermost" (Heb. 7:25)! That is life-changing news for the "chief of sinners." If Christ can save Paul, who was a blasphemer, a persecutor, and injurer of innocents, He can also save you, no matter how hell-worthy you may be. Ask Jesus Christ for the grace of repentance and faith that you may put all your trust in Him (cf. Acts 5:31).

TO BRING LIGHT TO
A DARK WORLD

I am come a light into the world, that whosoever believeth on me should not abide in darkness.
—JOHN 12:46

If I had not come and spoken unto them, they had not had sin: but now they have no cloak for their sin.
—JOHN 15:22

Bright light is a mixed blessing. While it frees us from the oppression of darkness, it also reveals the ugly flaws and imperfections that previously lay hidden in the shadows. As the light of the world, Christ reveals the rottenness of sin (John 9:5). Since the fall in Adam, God had sent prophets to expose people's sin, call them to repentance, and point them to Christ (Jer. 25:3–7). Nonetheless, sin's ghastliness was not made fully manifest until Christ came to earth (Acts 17:30; cf. Luke 12:48). Because they were sinners, none of God's earlier messengers had personally embodied the stark contrast between God's holiness and man's sinfulness. In Christ's suffering, particularly in the crucifixion, the darkest blot was painted on the brightest canvas.

Christ came as the brightness of God's glory, in true and complete innocence, to reveal the abominable character of sin (Heb. 1:3; cf. Ezek. 8:3–4). We often describe babies or young children as innocent, but in Psalm 51:5, the psalmist confesses, "Behold, I was shapen in iniquity; and in sin did my mother conceive me." Christ alone entered the world innocent. The Gospels highlight Jesus' innocence, particularly in the hours preceding His death. The Sanhedrin struggled in vain to find sufficient false witnesses to agree on a charge to lay against Him (Matt. 26:60). When the crowd demanded that Jesus be crucified, Pilate asked, "Why, what evil hath he done?" (Matt. 27:23). In the span of nine verses, John records Pilate saying three times that he can find no fault in Christ (John 18:38–19:6). The centurion in command of the soldiers who were to carry out Pilate's death sentence confirmed Christ's innocence, saying, "Certainly this was a righteous man" (Luke 23:47). Even creation revolted at the Innocent's unjust death; Matthew 27:51 says, "The earth did quake, and the rocks rent."

Christ came as the brightness of God's glory to reveal the abominable character of sin (Heb. 1:3; cf. Ezek. 8:3–4). The glory of the gospel is that the Innocent One not only exposes sin by His light, but He also delivers us from sin's darkness.

The world into which Jesus came, ruled by pagan Rome, lay in darkness. Even among God's people were few who practiced true religion. Many of the religious leaders had become blind guides (Matt. 23:24). True religion was like a single, flickering candle set against the dark, howling night. Seven hundred years before Christ's birth, Isaiah had said, "The people that walked in darkness have seen a great light: they that dwell in the land of the shadow of death, upon them hath the light shined" (9:2; cf. Luke 1:79).

Fittingly, the birth of Christ was heralded by the shining of bright light in a dark world. Suddenly, in the dark of night, the angel of the Lord stood before the shepherds, "and the glory of the Lord shone round about them" (Luke 2:9). Later, a bright star directed the Magi to Jesus (Matt. 2:1–12). A still more glorious light accompanied Jesus' life and ministry. The apostle John recalls beholding the glory of the Word made flesh (John 1:14). Jesus, the Light of the World, promised, "He that followeth me shall not walk in darkness, but shall have the light of life" (John 8:12). Shortly before His death Jesus said, "A little while is the light with you.... While ye have light, believe in the light, that ye may be the children of light" (John 12:35–36). When that light was lifted up at Golgotha, both the justice and redeeming love of God shone with burning brightness (cf. John 12:32).

We take light for granted until we are without it. The last time you tried to find your way in the darkness, you probably held your arms out as you groped for something firm. God is not far from any of us. The problem is simply that until He opens our eyes, we can't see Him but are left to "feel after Him" in the darkness (Acts 17:27). We can't make sense of our lives until "God, who commanded the light to shine out of darkness, hath shined in our hearts, to give the light of the knowledge of the glory of God in the face of Jesus Christ" (2 Cor. 4:6). As the pillar of fire who led His people through the wilderness (Ex. 13:21; 14:20), the Lord Jesus Christ has called out of darkness and into His marvelous light a "chosen generation, a royal priesthood, an holy nation, a peculiar people," to show forth His praises (1 Peter 2:9). Calvin says, "If the whole wisdom of the world were collected into one mass, not a single ray of the true light would be found in that vast heap; but, on the contrary, it will be found a confused chaos; for it belongs to Christ alone to deliver us from darkness."[1]

4

TO BE MADE LIKE HIS PEOPLE

> *Forasmuch then as the children are partakers of flesh and blood, he also himself likewise took part of the same.... For verily he took not on him the nature of angels; but he took on him the seed of Abraham. Wherefore in all things it behoved him to be made like unto his brethren.*
> —HEBREWS 2:14, 16–17

Christ came to earth as God to take upon Himself the flesh and blood of our human nature. That is a profound statement. The baby in the manger had the same human nature as you and I, only without sin. Jesus was born perfect. As the perfect man, our Lord Jesus represents the great hope for imperfect people. Sometimes little babies inspire the hope of a fresh start, and how much more this little baby, even when He was wrapped in swaddling clothes and lying in a manger.

In Christ's incarnation, God teaches us that we cannot solve our problems on our own. We cannot attain perfection and peace by our own strength. But in Christ, God has done it for us. In the words of church father Irenaeus of Lyon, "When He became incarnate, and was made man, He commenced afresh the long line of human beings, and furnished us, in a brief, comprehensive manner, with salvation; so that what we had lost in Adam—namely, to be according to the image and likeness of God—that we might recover in Christ Jesus."[1] Christ came to be like us so that His death would accomplish healing for us. Apart from a true incarnation, there is no true atonement.

Because He is like us, Christ also sympathizes with all the pains and miseries that come from living in a sin-afflicted world. The body that God prepared for the Son "groaneth and travaileth in pain" as our bodies do (Rom. 8:22). When His bodily strength was spent, He slept (Mark 4:38). When His heart broke with grief, He wept (John 11:35).

Because He is like us, we draw encouragement from Christ's steadfastness in the face of temptation. Hebrews 4:15 tells us, "For we have not an high priest which cannot be touched with the feeling of our infirmities; but was in all points tempted like as we are, yet without sin." The comfort in Christ's temptation is that He experienced the same temptations that we face, but He did not give in. As Christians, we sometimes struggle with painful doubts. We look at our sins, grieve over them, and wonder how we could possibly be saved. How easily we give in to temptation! At even the faintest scent of carnal indulgence, our mouths begin to water. We are discouraged by our failures. At such times we must take refuge in the temptations of Christ, because He passed the test! Our salvation does not depend on our performance but on Christ's. In His human obedience, we have a grand demonstration that Christ will never fail us. Christ did not come to earth simply to be our moral teacher. If that were His only mission, He could have come as He did in former times, as the Angel of the LORD, without our flesh and blood to encumber Him. Instead, He had to become like us so that He could raise us up to be like Him.

By faith, when we think of Christ, we should see ourselves in Him. As we glimpse at the manger of His birth we can say, "This is my brother, my flesh and blood." As He grows and matures and continues to do the will of God, we can say, "This is my brother, my flesh and blood." As He goes to the cross and bleeds and dies, we can say, "This is my brother, my flesh and blood." When we see Christ seated at the right hand of God the Father Almighty, we can say, "This is my brother, my flesh and blood." And when we see Christ return on clouds of glory to take us home to be with Him we will say, "This is my brother, my flesh and blood." Because of the incarnation, believers can say of Christ what Adam said of Eve—"This is now bone of my bones, and flesh of my flesh"—and what the apostle Paul says to the Ephesians: "We are members of his body, of his flesh, and of his bones" (5:30).

The writers of the Second Helvetic Confession (11.4) explain, "The flesh of Christ, therefore, was neither flesh in show only, nor yet flesh brought from heaven." Rather, the flesh of Christ is our flesh. "For both he that sanctifieth and they who are sanctified are all of one: for which cause he is not ashamed to call them brethren" (Heb. 2:11).

5

TO BEAR WITNESS
TO THE TRUTH

*Pilate therefore said unto him, Art thou a king then? Jesus
answered, Thou sayest that I am a king. To this end was I
born, and for this cause came I into the world, that I should
bear witness unto the truth. Every one that is of the truth
heareth my voice.*

—JOHN 18:37

During the Christmas season, people who give little thought
to Jesus Christ and His incarnation most of the year come
together, despite their radical differences. Many of them
would say that truth is relative—that what you believe to be
true may or may not be true for them, that there is more than
one way to God, and that your truth is not necessarily supe-
rior to theirs. But for a few weeks in December, people with
a variety of views—often contradictory—unify in the "spirit
of Christmas." Ironically, they are unknowingly celebrating
the coming of Jesus who, shortly before His death, declared
to Pilate that He had been born "to bear witness to *the* truth"
and, by implication, expose everything else as false.

In cultures and thought systems that reject the very idea
of absolute truth rooted in Christ, speaking the truth is
not necessarily a virtue, and lying is not necessarily a fault.
In Hinduism certain forms of lying, deceit, and theft are

considered virtuous. Today, even in Judeo-Christian contexts, people frequently question the existence of truth itself. Some people wonder whether truth matters. In a similarly relativistic culture two thousand years ago, the ultimate expression of truth appeared on this earth in the person of the Lord Jesus Christ. Standing before Pontius Pilate, Jesus declared, "For this cause I was born, and for this cause I have come into the world, that I should bear witness to the truth." Earlier He said, "I am the truth!" (John 14:6). Truth is intimately connected with Christ and His coming into the world.

When we think about Christ's coming, we should consider the truth to which Jesus' birth testifies. He came to testify that all men pervert the truth and justice of God. As Paul says in Romans 3:4, "Let God be true, but every man a liar." The truth of God in Christ shines light upon our hearts and exposes the lies we use to justify a life at odds with God. But He also came to address this problem. Christ bears witness to "the word of truth, the gospel of your salvation" (Eph. 1:13). When we look to Christ by faith, we are overwhelmed by the radical truthfulness of God and the radical deception that is found in each one of us (Deut. 32:4; Jer. 17:9). But we also begin to hear Christ teach the way of God in truth (Matt. 22:16). As we walk in this way, we will find great freedom.

Pilate questioned the existence of truth, and his life bore the fruit of his doubts. He lived in fear of losing his position. Against his conscience, he gave deference to the mad requests of the people. He disregarded the advice of his wife, who urged him to have nothing to do with Jesus' death. Pilate was in bondage because he didn't know the truth. Even though he spent many years bound in prison, the apostle Paul declares, "Stand fast...in the liberty wherewith Christ hath made us free" (Gal. 5:1). So you can be a prisoner and yet be truly free, or you can be a king and live in bondage. As Paul testified in chains before kings, it was clear that he, not they, knew true freedom (Acts 24:16, 25). You can almost hear the chains rattling on Pilate's wrists when he asks Jesus, "What is truth?" (John 18:38).

Jesus testifies, "Every one that is of the truth heareth my voice" (John 18:37) and promises that "the truth shall make you free" (John 8:32). Do you experience true freedom in Christ? Or are you living in bondage to the fear of men, to the demands of your flesh, and to the guilt of lies? As we experience salvation in Christ, we begin to see that truth and lies are like oil and water. In Christ we can reject everything that is false and begin to live freely in the truth. We find healing for our deceitful hearts in His truth. We learn to hate lies and deception because they attack Christ as surely as nails pierced His hands and feet. A tremendous series of lies sent Christ to the cross! We love the truth because it is a reflection of Jesus Christ, who is truth incarnate (John 14:6).

TO DESTROY THE DEVIL AND HIS WORKS

Forasmuch then as the children are partakers of flesh and blood, he also himself likewise took part of the same; that through death he might destroy him that had the power of death, that is, the devil.
—HEBREWS 2:14

He that committeth sin is of the devil; for the devil sinneth from the beginning. For this purpose the Son of God was manifested, that he might destroy the works of the devil.
—1 JOHN 3:8

The devil has always raged against God and His church, seeking her destruction (John 8:44). But Jesus' physical entry into the world heightened the intensity of the battle between God and Satan.

Satan remembered the words God had thundered at him in the garden of Eden: "And I will put enmity between thee and the woman, and between thy seed and her seed; it shall bruise thy head, and thou shalt bruise his heel" (Gen. 3:15). At Jesus' birth, the devil was poised to cut short the redeeming work of the woman's seed. Working through Herod, Satan tried to extinguish the Christ child's life before He reached His second birthday (Matt. 2:16).

The book of Revelation was written to encourage Christians with the good news that in the end, God would defeat the devil. In chapter 12, John saw Satan as a great red dragon standing before "the woman which was ready to be delivered, for to devour her child as soon as it was born" (vv. 3–4). In Revelation 20:10, however, John sees the dragon "cast into the lake of fire and brimstone, where the beast and the false prophet are, and shall be tormented day and night for ever and ever." This is the bitter end of the devil and his coworkers (Matt. 13:39–42; 25:41). Therefore, like a man on death row with no possibility of parole, Satan and his host, "to the utmost of their power as murderers [watch] to ruin the Church and every member thereof...daily expecting their horrible torments" (Belgic Confession, art. 12).

Therefore, as the devil rages we must not lose hope, for Christ came to destroy the devil's works. Throughout His earthly ministry, Jesus exercised dominion over the powers of hell. He fought the devil with the word as the sword of the Spirit (Matt. 4:1–11; Eph. 6:17). He "went about doing good, and healing all that were oppressed of the devil; for God was with him" (Acts 10:38). Before Christ's power the demons groveled in the dust, begging for mercy (Luke 8:31). When Jesus died on the cross, some of His followers feared that the devil had won. But with His death, Christ conquered death, the great enemy of mankind that had entered the world through Adam's sin (Rom. 5:12). It was the tool the devil used to keep men in fear and bondage (Heb. 2:14, 15). Yet with His death, Jesus crushed the serpent's head (Gen. 3:15). Indeed, Satan fell like lightning from heaven, but to no avail (Luke 10:18).

Reflecting on Christ's first coming helps us to remember Christ's devil-destroying work. Because He has conquered death, Jesus' disciples can resist the devil in His name (Eph. 6:11; James 4:7). They can say no to the works of the flesh, knowing that Christ came to destroy those as well. Believers have the freedom to obey God's command: "Let not sin therefore reign in your mortal body, that ye should obey it in the lusts thereof" (Rom. 6:12). We have the power to pray to Satan's slayer, "Order my steps in thy word: and let not any iniquity have dominion over me" (Ps. 119:133).

Christ's power over Satan and his works should give us great confidence. Imagine being one of the Israelites in the Valley of Elah in the days of King Saul. Every day the Philistine champion Goliath defied the people of Israel and their God. And every day they were "dismayed, and greatly afraid" (1 Sam. 17:11). But then imagine the joy of seeing God's warrior, David, slaying the giant and holding up his severed head. Later in that chapter, we learn that when the Israelites saw that Goliath was dead, they "arose, and shouted, and pursued the Philistines," plundering their tents (vv. 51–53). Christians have no reason to dwell in the valley of defeat, for Christ is our giant killer. In Him we also have power over the devil (Acts 13:9–12).

The great German pastor and hymn writer Johann Rist had this great victory in mind when he composed these words in 1641:

> Break forth, O beauteous heavenly light,
> And usher in the morning.
> O shepherds, shudder not with fright,
> But hear the angel's warning.
> This child, now weak in infancy,
> Our confidence and joy shall be,
> The power of Satan breaking,
> Our peace eternal making.
> —"Break Forth, O Beauteous Heavenly Light"

TO GIVE ETERNAL LIFE

I am the living bread which came down from heaven: if any man eat of this bread, he shall live forever: and the bread that I will give is my flesh, which I will give for the life of the world.

—JOHN 6:51

Our earthly bodies, which are corrupted by sin, are destined to grow old, decay, and die. All the money in the world cannot save us from natural corruption; we need a cure from heaven. In His incarnation, Christ provides that cure. He was sent into the world as the remedy for sinful flesh. Because His flesh was untainted by corruption, He could give His body as a ransom for the life we forfeited by sin. His life must be exchanged for ours so that we may be spared.

In startling fashion, Jesus teaches His disciples that, like physical bread and wine, His body and blood will bless those who feed on Him. He says in John 6:53–54, "Except ye eat the flesh of the Son of man, and drink his blood, ye have no life in you. Whoso eateth my flesh, and drinketh my blood, hath eternal life; and I will raise him up at the last day." He presents Himself as the food and drink of eternal life. Puritan Bible commentator Matthew Henry observed, "Everything else we eat is a shadow compared to Christ."

Believers must not just think or talk about Jesus; they must feast on Him. An old Latin hymn puts it this way:

> We taste Thee, O Thou living bread,
> And long to feast upon Thee still;
> We drink of Thee, the fountainhead,
> And thirst our souls from Thee to fill.[1]

How do we feast on Him? We should clarify that Christ was not teaching us to be cannibals. The sixth commandment imparts sanctity to human life that must not be violated. Thus, Christ's language in John 6 refers not to a physical act but to the spiritual act of feeding on Him in our hearts by faith.

First, we develop an appetite for Christ by committing our hearts to Him, knowing that only He can satisfy our deepest longings. We learn to say of Christ, "Thou art my God; early will I seek thee: my soul thirsteth for thee, my flesh longeth for thee in a dry and thirsty land, where no water is…. My soul shall be satisfied as with marrow and fatness; and my mouth shall praise thee with joyful lips" (Ps. 63:1, 5).

Second, we meditate upon Him. We must recollect and reflect on all that we learn of Christ. We reflect on His names, His states, His works, and His words. Then we apply every "bite" of His person and work to our lives.

Third, we delight in Him. God gave us food not only to strengthen us physically but also to cheer us. Christ is not just the food we need; He is also the food that we desire and our portion forever (Ps. 73:25–26). We cry out with the psalmist, "O taste and see that the LORD is good: blessed is the man that trusteth in him" (Ps. 34:8).

Finally, we feed upon Him regularly. Our bodies must be fed daily to maintain our health and strength. When God rained down manna in the wilderness, His people had to gather it daily (Ex. 16:4–5). Some of us have little spiritual vitality because we fail to feed on Christ day by day. Over time, we become spiritually anorexic. We should realize that every part of Scripture speaks of Christ (John 5:39). Thus, every time we read a passage of God's Word, we should ask how it bears witness to Him. We make Christ our favorite daily food.

When we sit down for a meal, we should eat what is good for our bodies. With God's blessing, our daily bread will sustain us. Something similar happens when we feed on Christ by faith. In article 35, the Belgic Confession explains the analogy between earthly and heavenly bread: "For the support of the spiritual and heavenly life which believers have, He hath sent a living bread which descended from heaven, namely, Jesus Christ, who nourishes and strengthens the spiritual life of believers when they eat Him, that is to say, when they apply and receive Him by faith in the Spirit."

This teaching has often been misunderstood, and Christians in the early church were persecuted because of the erroneous belief that they were cannibals and celebrated secret feasts at which they ate human flesh and drank human blood. In a certain sense this was true; while Christians were not eating and drinking physical flesh and blood, they were spiritually eating and drinking, for the Belgic Confession explains that, in the Lord's Supper, "what is eaten and drunk by us is the proper and natural body and the proper blood of Christ. But the manner of our partaking of the same is not by the mouth, but by the Spirit through faith."

To benefit from eating the Bread of Life, the Bread must first be broken. Christ's body was broken on the cross so that we could share in His life. Truly Christ came to give us eternal life.

TO RECEIVE WORSHIP

Now when Jesus was born in Bethlehem of Judaea in the days of Herod the king, behold, there came wise men from the east to Jerusalem, saying, Where is he that is born King of the Jews? for we have seen his star in the east, and are come to worship him.... And when they were come into the house, they saw the young child with Mary his mother, and fell down, and worshipped him: and when they had opened their treasures, they presented unto him gifts; gold, and frankincense and myrrh.

—MATTHEW 2:1–2, 11

What a privilege the wise men had! They were the first Gentiles to see Christ in the flesh. In fulfillment of David's prophecy in Psalm 22:27–30, they worshiped the Christ child and gave Him gifts:

All the ends of the world shall remember and turn unto the LORD: and all the kindreds of the nations shall worship before thee. For the kingdom is the LORD's: and he is the governor among the nations. All they that be fat upon earth shall eat and worship: all they that go down to the dust shall bow before him: and none can keep alive his own soul. A seed shall serve him; it shall be accounted to the Lord for a generation.

The wise men understood that Christ came to be worshiped. Though Christ is not physically with us today, we must still worship Him. We must follow the example of Christ's disciples who witnessed His ascension into heaven and then responded by bowing before Him in adoration. As Luke 24:52 says, "They worshipped him."

These wise men from the East can teach us how to worship Christ today. To worship Christ, we must first seek Him as the wise men did. As the Magi sought Christ with a sense of urgency, we must also "seek...the LORD while he may be found" (Isa. 55:6). We do not seek Christ in a stable in Bethlehem; rather, we seek Him in heaven, where He reigns at the right hand of God. Christ came to earth to live, minister, die, rise from death, and ascend to heaven, where He draws us to Himself. God drew the wise men to Bethlehem by means of a star. But Christ Himself is our bright and morning star (2 Peter 1:19; Rev. 22:16), and His Word and Spirit still draw lost sinners to God. God works in our hearts to make us seekers after Christ (Ps. 27:8) instead of hiders from God (Gen. 3:8). The most important way to seek Christ is in the public worship of His church. The writer of Hebrews makes the startling observation that while the Israelites left Egypt to worship God at Mount Sinai, New Testament believers gather together "unto mount Sion, and unto the city of the living God, the heavenly Jerusalem, and to an innumerable company of angels, to the general assembly and church of the firstborn, which are written in heaven, and to God the Judge of all, and to the spirits of just men made perfect, and to Jesus the mediator of the new covenant, and to the blood of sprinkling, that speaketh better things than that of Abel" (12:22–24).

Second, in worshiping Christ, we find joy in Him. We are told that as the wise men sought Christ, they "rejoiced with exceeding great joy" (Matt. 2:10). Christ's advent, in particular, teaches us the joy of anticipating Jesus. The Christian journey is riddled with trials and difficulties, but the brilliance of the One whom we seek turns our mourning into dancing (Ps. 30:11). Isaiah 35:10 tells us, "The ransomed of the LORD shall return, and come to Zion with songs and everlasting joy on their heads: they shall obtain joy and gladness, and sorrow and sighing shall flee away" (Isa. 35:10). And Colossians 1:24 says that those whose chief end is to glorify God and enjoy Him forever can rejoice even in sufferings. Because fellowship with Christ is both our goal and present reality, we find joy in the journey to Christ as well as in the arrival at the destination.

Third, in worshiping Christ we present gifts to Him as the wise men did. We ask as the psalmist did: "What shall I render unto the LORD for all his benefits toward me?" (Ps. 116:12). More precious, though, than the Magi's gold, frankincense, and myrrh is a broken and contrite heart (Ps. 51:17), true faith (1 Peter 1:7), new obedience (1 Thess. 4:1–3), and sacrifices of praise (Heb. 13:15). A truly wise person submits to the hand of God and devotes himself and everything he has to his Lord and Savior. As we offer our gifts to Christ, we should be mindful of God's grace, for our gifts to God begin as His gifts to us. As Augustine says, when God rewards our good deeds, He "doth crown in us, not our deserts, but His own gifts."[1] In his reflection on the incarnation, the Dutch Further Reformation divine Wilhelmus à Brakel wrote:

> If the Lord Jesus is God, meditation upon Him as such will generate great reverence in our hearts, and cause us

to exalt Him far above everything. It will cause us to bow before Him, to worship Him with the angels, to honor Him as the Father, He being one with Him; and we will join all creatures in heaven and upon earth by exclaiming, "Blessing, and honour, and glory, and power, be unto Him that sitteth upon the throne, and unto the Lamb for ever and ever" (Rev. 5:13).[2]

Christ came to receive such worship, for He is altogether worthy of it. Are you a true worshiper of the Lamb?

TO BRING GREAT JOY

And the angel said unto them, Fear not: for, behold, I bring
you good tidings of great joy, which shall be to all people.
—LUKE 2:10

With due respect to President Franklin D. Roosevelt, not
all fear is to be feared. Some fear is perfectly rational. For
example, it's understandable that the shepherds were fright-
ened the night God announced the birth of His Son. They
had been minding their own business, "keeping watch over
their flock by night" (Luke 2:8), when suddenly the darkness was shattered by a great light. Right before their faces
stood the angel of the Lord. Luke says the shepherds were
"sore afraid" (2:9). How fitting it is, then, that in the next
verse the angel announced "good tidings of great joy" (2:10).
Jesus came to turn great fear into great joy.

The Old Testament prophecies about the coming Messiah resound with joy. Isaiah anticipated that those who
heard of Christ's birth would rejoice "according to the joy
in harvest, and as men rejoice when they divide the spoil....
For unto us a child is born, unto us a son is given" (Isa. 9:3,
6). The saints who had looked forward to the coming of
Christ could then say, "We have waited for him, and he will

save us; this is the LORD; we have waited for him, we will be glad and rejoice in his salvation" (Isa. 25:9). Jesus Himself said, "I tell you, that many prophets and kings have desired to see those things which ye see" (Luke 10:24).

Throughout His earthly ministry, Jesus fulfilled this reason for His coming. John the Baptist, who would endure so much suffering at the hands of wicked men for the sake of Jesus, said of Him: "He that hath the bride is the bridegroom: but the friend of the bridegroom, which standeth and heareth him, rejoiceth greatly because of the bridegroom's voice: this my joy therefore is fulfilled" (John 3:29). The very sound of Jesus' voice brought joy to John the Baptist's heart. Even before he was born, John leaped for joy in his mother's womb (Luke 1:44).

Near the end of Jesus' earthly ministry, when the cross loomed darkly over the heads of Him and His disciples, the message of joy pierced the darkness. Jesus reminded His disciples of the unshakable love God has for His own, saying, "As the Father hath loved me, so have I loved you: continue ye in my love" (John 15:9). Jesus then helped His disciples apply this great truth of His abiding love: "These things I have spoken unto you, that my joy might remain in you, and that your joy might be full" (John 15:11).

In Luke's gospel, fear turns to joy in the announcement of Jesus' birth. Interestingly, the same thing happens in Luke 24:37 when the resurrected Jesus suddenly appears in the midst of the disciples. Initially, they are "terrified and affrighted," but a few verses later, they are overcome with joy (24:41). Luke closes his gospel account with these words: "And they worshipped him, and returned to Jerusalem with great joy: and were continually in the temple, praising and blessing God" (24:52–53; cf. John 16:20–24). Christ filled His disciples with the kind of joy that conquers even the sadness of a dear friend's death.

Jesus came to earth to bring true joy and explain where it may be found. People look for joy in food, drink, friends, family, work, and recreation. As believers, we find some satisfaction in these things. But because the things of this world are fleeting, we may not seek ultimate joy in them, and neither should they move us to great despair. Indeed, Christians should expect the world *not* to satisfy them. C. S. Lewis reflected, "If we find ourselves with a desire that nothing in this world can satisfy, the most probable explanation is that we were made for another world."[1] And while we're in this world, we must expect to find joy in the otherworldly, for Romans 14:17 says, "The kingdom of God is not meat and drink; but righteousness, and peace, and joy in the Holy Ghost."

Few of us have ever received a gift that we would truly describe as unspeakable or indescribable. Some gifts are better than others, but usually we can describe them. In 2 Corinthians 9, Paul writes about Christ's incarnation. At the end of the chapter he says, "Thanks be to God for his unspeakable gift" (v. 15). Even Paul, a gifted wordsmith, could not put the wonder of this gift into words! As we reflect on the incarnation, we too should be filled with joyous amazement and thanksgiving. Wilhelmus à Brakel explains, "The reason one does not rejoice in the incarnation is for lack of holy meditation upon the subject, its miraculous nature, the promises, the Person, the fruits and this great salvation brought about by His suffering and death. What reason for rejoicing would he who does not attentively reflect upon this have?"[2]

TO DEMONSTRATE TRUE HUMILITY

Let this mind be in you, which was also in Christ Jesus: who, being in the form of God, thought it not robbery to be equal with God: but made himself of no reputation, and took upon him the form of a servant, and was made in the likeness of men: and being found in fashion as a man, he humbled himself, and became obedient unto death, even the death of the cross.

—PHILIPPIANS 2:5–8

Philippians 2:3–4 commands us to be humble: "Let nothing be done through strife or vainglory; but in lowliness of mind let each esteem other better than themselves. Look not every man on his own things, but every man also on the things of others." The word *humble*, which literally means "low," is from the Latin *humus*, meaning "earth" or "of the earth." Thus, to be humble is to be "down to earth." Humbling someone makes a person low, reduces him to meaner circumstances, or assigns him to a lower rank or place. We humble ourselves by behaving in an unassuming manner, by placing others before us, by judging ourselves more strictly than others, and by magnifying the good in others rather than in ourselves. God commands us to humble ourselves before Him and before our fellow human beings.

But what does humility actually look like in practice? How often do we witness true humility in action? Though humility was rigorously commanded throughout the entire Old Testament age, no one had ever witnessed a perfect example of humility (Micah 6:8). Even Moses, whom Scripture calls the meekest man on earth, was not always humble (Num. 12:3; 20:11–12).

Then Christ was born. At His birth humility assumed flesh and blood. If humiliation means to reduce oneself to a lower status for the sake of others, no one has done that more than Jesus. Spurgeon said that in the incarnation of Christ, "God's omnipotence cometh down to man's feebleness, and infinite majesty stoops to man's infirmity." In Christ "the infinite became an infant."[1] C. S. Lewis uses cosmic language to say that in the incarnation "God has landed on this enemy-occupied planet in human form."[2]

In instructing us to be humble, Paul offers a living, breathing example of humility. He says, "Let this mind be in you, which was also in Christ Jesus" (Phil. 2:5). Paul reminds us in verse 8 that Jesus, who was in the form of God, humbled Himself. That is one of the greatest understatements of all time. Christ could have come from no higher position, and He could have descended to none lower. Though He existed in the form of God, He consented to become a man. He not only became a man, He became a common man. As the Westminster Larger Catechism says, He was "made of a woman of low estate, and… born of her; with divers circumstances of more than ordinary abasement" (Q. 47). He not only became a common man, He willfully served other common men, even bowing to wash their dusty feet.

No task was beneath Christ's dignity as the Servant of the Lord. He not only served other men, but He also gave His life for them. He not only gave His life, but He also did so on a cross, an instrument of death accursed of God. While hanging on that cross, He descended into hell, bearing our sins and shame. He willfully gave up His position of glory at the right hand of His Father to become the object of His Father's righteous wrath against sin. Much more than the first Adam, Christ experienced the bitterness of stepping out of Paradise into a corrupt and hostile world (Rom. 5:12–21).

Without the example of Christ, we might fabricate all sorts of ways to minimize the call to be humble. But in His coming to earth, Christ exposes all of our objections to humility as wicked pride. Faced with the demands of humility, we can never say to God, "You don't know what it's like to stoop *this* low!" Christ came to demonstrate true humility. So Paul says, "Let *this* mind be in you, which was also in Christ Jesus."

But Christ also humbled Himself so that He could later be exalted. When Jesus said, "Blessed are the meek: for they shall inherit the earth" (Matt. 5:5), He was first of all talking about Himself (Matt. 11:29). But He was also including believers, for in God's economy, the way up is down. Jesus promises, "Whosoever therefore shall humble himself as [a] little child, the same is the greatest in the kingdom of heaven" (Matt. 18:14). Humble yourself so that God will one day lift you up to heights of glory that are presently unimaginable (cf. James 4:10; 1 Peter 5:6).

TO PREACH THE GOSPEL

The Spirit of the Lord is upon me, because he hath anointed me to preach the gospel to the poor; he hath sent me to heal the brokenhearted, to preach deliverance to the captives, and recovering of sight to the blind, to set at liberty them that are bruised.... And he said unto them, I must preach the king-dom of God to other cities also: for therefore am I sent.
—LUKE 4:18, 43; cf. ISAIAH 61:1–2

Isaiah prophesied during a time of steep decline in the spiri-tuality of God's people. It was a dark time in which Israel had forsaken her God. Though they were outwardly pros-perous, the people indulged themselves in the pleasures of the world rather than show gratitude to God for those blessings. For that reason Isaiah was commanded to pro-nounce God's judgment on Israel. In the fullness of time, God would send the Assyrian army to devastate the coun-tryside of Judah and besiege Jerusalem. In 722 BC many Israelites from the northern kingdom were carried into exile in Assyria, never to return.

In the midst of this fearful prophecy, God also told Isaiah to give the people hope (chapters 40–66). According to the word of the Lord, Isaiah predicted the fall of the oppressors of God's people and said that a remnant of them would one day return to the Promised Land. He challenged that remnant to remain loyal to the Lord upon their return. Truly Isaiah could say, "The Spirit of the Lord GOD is upon me; because the LORD hath anointed me to preach good tidings unto the meek" (Isa. 61:1). But Isaiah was not just speaking about himself in this prophecy, nor was His good news only for the poor people living in the era of the divided kingdom.

More than seven hundred years after Isaiah, a relatively obscure carpenter's son from the small town of Nazareth walked into His hometown synagogue on the Sabbath day and stood to read. He was handed the scroll of Isaiah. He opened the book and read the prophecy about the one who had the Spirit of the Lord upon Him and was anointed to preach the gospel to the poor. He read a few more lines, closed the book, handed it back to the attendant, and sat down to teach. The eyes of everyone in the synagogue were fastened on Him, especially when He said, "This day is this scripture fulfilled in your ears" (Luke 4:21). The one whom the Spirit had anointed to preach the gospel was here. It was Jesus.

Jesus came to earth to be anointed to preach, or to proclaim with authority, the gospel to the poor. Like those who listened to Isaiah's message, Jesus' audience needed to hear good news. Although they were in their own land, Israel was subjugated by the Romans. The good news that Jesus proclaimed was not that the Romans would be overthrown (although eventually that would happen) but that He had come to rescue sinners from sin and themselves.

After hearing this passage read at family worship, a young child might ask the question, "If Jesus came to preach the gospel to the *poor*, did He come to preach to us? We're not poor." Of course, both princes and paupers can be poor, for all of mankind has lost everything due to Adam's sin in the garden of Eden.

Prior to the fall, man, as God's image bearer, reflected the wisdom, righteousness, and holiness of God. According to the Canons of Dort, "His understanding was adorned with a true and saving knowledge of his Creator, and of spiritual things" (III–IV, 1). Adam knew God. He walked and talked with Him. His heart and will were upright and positively inclined toward his Creator. He agreed with God. All his affections were pure. Adam had no mixed motives. Resisting sin was easy. Certainly he had to resist the fruit of the forbidden tree, but his resistance was not like that of a believer today who agonizes over temptation. In his original condition, man was inclined not to sin. How rich he was!

How poor we are! Our sins have exiled us from God. By nature we are prone to hate God and our neighbor. We need to hear the good news that Christ came to preach to us. We need to appreciate the beauty of "the feet of him that bringeth good tidings, that publisheth peace; that bringeth good tidings of good, that publisheth salvation; that saith unto Zion, Thy God reigneth!" (Isa. 52:7). In Psalm 40:10, David envisions Christ preaching to His people, and we need to hear Him:

> Before Thy people I confess
> The wonders of Thy righteousness;
> Thou knowest, Lord, that I have made
> Thy great salvation known,
> Thy truth and faithfulness displayed,
> Thy lovingkindness shown.
>
> —versification of Psalm 40:10,
> *The Psalter*, no. 112:1

12

TO BRING JUDGMENT

*And Jesus said, For judgment I am come into this world, that
they which see not might see; and that they which see might
be made blind. And some of the Pharisees which were with
him heard these words, and said unto him, are we blind also?
Jesus said unto them, If ye were blind, ye should have no sin:
but now ye say, We see; therefore your sin remaineth.*

—JOHN 9:39–41

Can you imagine a Christmas card quoting Jesus' words in
John 9:39: "For judgment I am come into this world"? It
probably would not be a best seller.

Today, judging others is unpopular. "Don't judge me"
has become a standard defense for questionable behavior. In
various ways, seemingly judgmental Christians are asked,
"Who are you to judge me?" People who know very little
about the Bible can still cite Jesus' words from the Sermon
on the Mount: "Judge not, that ye be not judged" (Matt.
7:1). We could describe people today with the ominous
refrain from the book of Judges: "Every man did that which
was right in his own eyes" (17:6). Some people in a self-
defensive posture are even bold enough to say, "God alone
is my judge."

On the other hand, some people naively assert, "My God doesn't judge." And some texts, carelessly read, seem to agree. In John 12, Jesus says that He came as light into a dark world. He then says, "And if any man hear my words, and believe not, I judge him not: for I came not to judge the world, but to save the world." But He goes on to say, "He that rejecteth me, and receiveth not my words, hath one that judgeth him: the word that I have spoken, the same shall judge him in the last day" (vv. 47–48).

Over the span of four chapters, John records Jesus saying both "I came not to judge the world" and "for judgment I am come into this world." Of course, both statements are true. Judgment means to divide truth from error as well as to uphold the good and condemn the wrong. Light makes a judgment by exposing what has been hidden in the dark. It forces us to face reality. In a dimly lit room, you don't notice stained carpet or peeling wallpaper. You also miss the beauty of crown molding around the ceiling. Christ's presence in the flesh and preaching of the gospel expose the sinful condition of humanity and force judgment upon what otherwise might be disregarded by men, at least for a time.

But that isn't all. According to Calvin, Christ also "lays aside for a time the office of a judge, and offers salvation to all without reserve, and stretches out His arms to embrace all, that all may be encouraged to repent."[1] In the words of Jesus Himself, "God sent not his Son into the world to condemn the world; but that the world through him might be saved. He that believeth on him is not condemned: but he that believeth not is condemned already, because he hath not believed in the name of the only begotten Son of God" (John 3:17–18). Christ's first coming to earth was a gracious harbinger of the upcoming day of judgment. It is a kind reminder that at least for today, the time of judgment has not yet come (Heb. 3:13; 4:7).

One reason Jesus appears to have opposing views on judgment is because of the different audiences to whom He speaks. In John 9, Jesus is preaching to the Pharisees, who have hardened their hearts against Him in unbelief. To them Jesus says, "For judgment I am come into this world." He is forcing such unbelievers to consider the judgment of God, which comes with cursing (Isa. 34:5), condemnation (Rom. 5:16), fear (Heb. 10:27), severity (James 2:13), and destruction (2 Peter 3:7). By contrast, in John 12, Jesus speaks to people who believe in Him but, because of the threat of the Pharisees to put them out of the synagogue, do not confess Him (v. 42). That had already happened to the man whom Jesus cured of blindness (John 9:34). To this audience Jesus cries out, confronting them with their guilt and urging them to believe in Him and no longer walk in darkness so they will not be judged by His word on the last day.

Christ is still judging people today. He gives sight to the blind and takes away the sight of those who claim to see truth but do not. What is your response to Jesus, the Light of the World? Are you a weak, struggling believer who draws strength from the light of Christ's coming? Or have you hardened your heart in unbelief and in the vain confidence of self-righteousness? To the latter Christ says, "For judgment I am come into this world."

TO GIVE HIS LIFE A RANSOM FOR MANY

For even the Son of man came not to be ministered unto, but to minister, and to give his life a ransom for many.

—MARK 10:45

Our Saviour Jesus Christ…gave himself for us, that he might redeem us from all iniquity, and purify unto himself a peculiar people, zealous of good works.

—TITUS 2:13–14

When we hear about a kidnapping, our hearts break. Imagine the horror, then, of discovering that someone you love has been kidnapped. You hear nothing about your loved one for days or even weeks. Then you receive a handwritten note in the mail. He will be freed if you leave one hundred thousand dollars in a certain location at a stated time. Your mind begins to swirl. Of course you will try to meet the demand for ransom. But how will you come up with that much money? How can you be sure that the ransom will be accepted and your loved one will be set free?

The Bible says that in Adam, all human beings have been kidnapped and held captive by sin, but Christ has come to earth to redeem His people by giving His life as a ransom. To *redeem* means "to buy back." In redemption a price is paid to free a person from the power of another. As nineteenth-century theologian Charles Hodge says, "Redemption is deliverance though the purchase price of the blood of Christ, from the power and consequences of sin."[1] As we consider Christ's ministry of redemption, we should ask the following questions.

First, from what are believers redeemed? The Bible answers this question two ways. First, it says that Christ redeems His people from Satan, who has snared the ungodly to do his will (2 Tim. 2:26). The Heidelberg Catechism says, "With his precious blood [Christ] has fully satisfied" the price of God's justice "for all my sins and delivered me from all the power of the devil" (Q. 1). That is good news! In *Pilgrim's Progress,* Apollyon and Christian faced each other in the Valley of Humiliation. Initially, Apollyon believed that Christian was still one of his subjects. But Christian now belonged to another master, the King of princes, and Satan no longer has a claim on God's believing children.

At the same time, the Bible says that unbelievers are captive to the curse of God's law because of their sins. This captivity is especially burdensome because it was justly imposed on us by an offended Creator. Jesus describes it in the plainest terms: "Whosoever committeth sin is the [slave] of sin" (John 8:34). Unbelievers are perpetual law-breakers (Rom. 14:23). Lawlessness has taken them hostage, and they cannot escape from this enemy. Fallen man needs to be emancipated from slavery. Christ came to redeem us from such captivity.

Second, by what are believers redeemed? Christ Himself paid the ransom for our sins. Christ became a man to purchase His church with His own blood (Acts 20:28). He gave

Himself for us, dying in our stead, that He might redeem us. Christ consented to be punished by God for all of our lawlessness. He could offer Himself as ransom because He was not a slave to sin. Christ can also redeem us from lawlessness because He is the perfect law keeper. That is why the obedience of Christ is so important to our redemption. In Psalm 69:4, David prophecies that Christ will say, "Then I restored that which I took not away" as the just one who makes restitution for the unjust. God redeems us by accepting the death of His dear Son in our place.

Finally, for what are believers redeemed? In a word, Christ redeems us to be obedient. Romans 6:18 says, "Being then made free from sin, ye became the servants of righteousness." In Christ we have both the desire and ability to keep God's law. Our freedom in Christ, therefore, obliges us to walk in the light of God's law as the expression of His holy will for our lives.

In redemption Christ purchases us for Himself. Believers belong to Christ (2 Cor. 5:14–15) as His "peculiar people" (Titus 2:14), which is another way of saying that we are His and His alone. In redemption Christ becomes our Savior and Lord. If you have been redeemed, you have a new master to whom you owe eternal loyalty.

Three times Apollyon promised Christian that if he would return to the City of Destruction and serve him, all would be well. Christian saw through that lie: "I have given [Christ] my faith and sworn allegiance to him…. And besides (O thou destroying Apollyon) to speak Truth, I like His Service, His Wages, His Servants, His Government, His Company, and Country, better than thine; and therefore leave off to persuade me further, I am His servant, and

I will follow Him."[2] If we have been bought by God, serving Him is our delight.

Suppose there was a kidnapping in your town, and the victim was a very rebellious child from an utterly dysfunctional family. The ransom note didn't ask for one hundred thousand dollars; it asked for your child in exchange for the bad kid. You would not agree to such an exchange. But Christ came to give His life as a ransom for rebellious, dysfunctional children like you and me.

TO FULFILL THE LAW
AND PROPHETS

*Think not that I am come to destroy the law, or the prophets:
I am not come to destroy, but to fulfil.* —MATTHEW 5:17

The Greek word for *fulfill* means to fill, complete, carry out, or perform. To fulfill a prophecy is to carry out in practice what was predicted. To fulfill the law is to obey its commands and put its precepts into practice. In Matthew 5, Christ says that before His coming to earth, the law and prophets were like unfilled jars. They didn't have holes in them or any other defects. The problem was that the water inside the jar never could make it to the top.

Since God is righteous, His kingdom is defined by righteousness. He requires, then, that everyone obey His moral law by "filling up the jar of righteousness." If they do not, they will perish. The righteousness that God requires is defined in His law and expounded by prophets such as Micah, who says, "He hath shewed thee, O man, what is good; and what doth the LORD require of thee, but to do justly, and to love mercy, and to walk humbly with thy God?" (6:8).

In Matthew 5:17 Jesus is speaking to the scribes and Pharisees, who were strict observers of Jewish tradition. Although they believed the law was valid, they fell far short of fulfilling it by turning precepts into practice. They were content to live by their traditions and customs, which often contradicted the law. Jesus condemned their emphasis on external, ceremonial cleanliness at the expense of the internal, loving reality of heartfelt obedience and holiness. He says salvation will come only to those whose righteousness exceeds that of the scribes and Pharisees. Jesus' listeners knew that no one could possibly fit that description.

But Jesus Christ fit that description. God did not change His righteous requirements when Christ came. Instead, when Christ came, He filled up the jar of the law and fulfilled all its requirements. He did so in two ways.

First, Christ and His atoning work were foreshadowed in the sacrifices and other ceremonies of the law. The law prophetically communicated the glory of the incarnate Christ. According to the apostle Paul, the law is like a trail that terminates in Christ: "For Christ is the end of the law for righteousness to everyone that believeth" (Rom. 10:4). In his commentary on this text, Calvin says that it is a "remarkable passage, which proves that the law in all its parts had a reference to Christ." He explains that the law was given "to lead us as by the hand to another righteousness. Whatever the law teaches, whatever it commands, whatever it promises, has always a reference to Christ as its main object; and hence all its part ought to be applied to Him." Before He ascended to heaven, Christ confirmed that in His sufferings, death, and resurrection He fulfilled the testimony of the law and the prophets concerning Him. It couldn't have been done any other way (Luke 24:44, 46).

At the same time, Christ fulfilled the law by doing everything that the law requires. From heaven, Christ breathed out the words of Psalm 119:44: "So shall I keep thy law continually for ever and ever." On earth, He put those words into practice. For the first time in human history, a man lived a rich and full life, "not only according to some, but all the commandments of God" (Heidelberg Catechism, Q. 114). This fulfillment of the law involved not only what Christ said and did but also what He suffered to satisfy the justice of God regarding sin.

Jesus also came to fulfill the prophets, whose ministry could be only an attempt to fill up the jar. They had spoken for God, declaring His will to the people, reminding them of the requirements of the law and the conditions of God's covenant and calling them to repent and return to the Lord. But one prophet after another had to repeat that message because so few people heeded the call to repent. Israel persisted in sin. The prophets also communicated God's judgment against His chosen people for failing to do His will. He sent judgment after judgment in fulfillment of the prophets' warnings. The last book of the Old Testament ends with the word *curse,* as though the prophet offered up one last reminder to warn Israel of God's wrath against sin before all the prophets fell silent for about four hundred years.

Finally, the prophets spoke for God by promising God's grace and forgiveness to repentant sinners. Throughout their ministry, the prophets had offered comfort to God's people, which was only a promise of better things yet to come. The jar of prophetic ministry was never filled up, though, because the final prophet had not yet come.

Christ is the final prophet, as Hebrews 1:1–2 makes clear: "God, who at sundry times and in divers manners spake in time past unto the fathers by the prophets, hath in these last days spoken unto us by his Son." Jesus both declared the will of God and performed it. He warned people about the judgment of God, and then endured that judgment for His people. He then promised eternal comfort by shedding His precious blood for them. Jesus came to fulfill the law and the prophets. He was the only one who could fill the jar of the law and the prophets! What was only potential has now become reality; what was only hoped for has now come to pass.

Wilhelmus à Brakel said, "The incarnation manifests the infallible veracity of God."[1] The first promise of salvation that God made to the first Adam came true in the second Adam (Gen. 3:15). Because of Christ's incarnation we have the fulfillment of this hope: "All the promises of God in him are yea, and in him Amen, unto the glory of God by us" (2 Cor. 1:20). In Christ the law has been fulfilled completely. In Him, it has become tangible and real for everyone to see. We may proclaim:

> Thy wondrous testimonies, Lord,
> My soul shall keep and greatly praise;
> Thy word, by faithful lips proclaimed,
> To simplest minds the truth conveys.
>
> Direct my footsteps in Thy word,
> From sin's dominion set me free,
> From man's oppression set me free,
> That I may yield to Thy control.

> —versification of Psalm 119:129–30, 133–34,
> *The Psalter*, no. 337:1, 3

15

TO REVEAL GOD'S
LOVE FOR SINNERS

*For God so loved the world, that he gave his only begotten
Son, that whosoever believeth in him should not perish, but
have everlasting life.*

—JOHN 3:16

John 3:16 has become so familiar that we no longer find its
words astonishing. But this remarkable Bible verse reveals an
amazing truth that should delight us every time we hear it.

John 3:16 makes the surprising claim that God loves the
world. God, the maker of heaven and earth, is self-suffi-
cient and needs nothing outside of Himself. He is the Holy
One whose pure eyes cannot look upon sin (Hab. 1:13). His
desires are always upright, His love completely pure, and
His affection never misplaced. How can such a God love the
broken, sin-marred world?

In the broadest sense, the world represents the universe
that God created. God loves the creation that He brought
into existence by His word. His love for the sin-corrupted
world is bound up in His plan to totally restore heaven and
earth (Acts 3:21).

More specifically, the world represents the human
inhabitants of the earth, the human race filled with rebels,
traitors, and idolaters. These objects of God's affection are

Why Christ Came

far from being worthy of God's love. Because man sinned, God would have done no injustice by letting us all perish (Rom. 3:19). Instead, God chose to love us.

Christ uses the word *world* to show the mystery and fullness of God's love, which is not limited to people of one race or to those who lived at a particular time or place. Note that Jesus does *not* speak of universal atonement here. He says He died for those whom God chose to believe in Him (John 6:37) and in whom He works saving faith as a gift of grace (Eph. 2:8). Still, God loves sinners and has provided a way of salvation for them through faith in His Son, Jesus Christ. John 3:16 affirms the certainty of God's love.

God's love for the world seems incongruous, far-fetched, and even impossible. To believe in this love, we need irrefutable evidence. Jesus' coming to the world is the irrefutable evidence of the Father's love for it. People can talk about their love for others, but the proof of love is action, not words (1 John 3:18). The apostle Paul speaks of Christ's death for us as proof of God's love, asserting, "God commendeth his love toward us, in that, while we were yet sinners, Christ died for us" (Rom. 5:8).

John 3:16 also reveals the riches of God's love. The kind of love God showed the world was not sentimental but sacrificial. It was *agape*, a committed and costly affection proved in action. It was "love, no matter what." According to John, only one event in the history of the world is capable of demonstrating true love. He writes, "Herein is love, not that we loved God, but that he loved us, and sent his Son to be the propitiation for our sins" (1 John 4:10).

God's love for His people can only be understood in relation to His love for His Son. The only begotten Son is the eternal object of the Father's affection. Two times during Christ's public ministry, the Father shattered heaven's silence to affirm His love for His Son (Matt. 3:17; 17:5). It is impossible to imagine the depth of love that binds the Father and the Son. Our love for our children is diminished by both our sin and theirs. Even the love of Jesus' earthly family and friends for Him was limited (Mark 3:21; John 7:5). But the love between God the Father and God the Son is perfect, personal, intimate, deep, and committed. It is love without limits, which is not subject to change or decay.

Christ came to earth to show us the riches of God's love. This is the good news of Christ's advent. In Jesus Christ, God loves His believing children with this same incomprehensible, infinite, and unchangeable love. The Father sent His Son to earth where He would die on the cross to deliver us from sin. Is it possible that He will now withhold from us any good thing (Rom. 8:32)? No, for Christ's incarnation confirms that nothing "shall be able to separate us from the love of God, which is in Christ Jesus our Lord" (Rom. 8:39).

16

TO CALL SINNERS
TO REPENTANCE

When Jesus heard it, he saith unto them, They that are whole have no need of the physician, but they that are sick: I came not to call the righteous, but sinners to repentance.

—MARK 2:17; cf. MATTHEW 9:13

One day Jesus passed by a tax office and saw a man named Matthew, a tax collector, and said, "Follow me" (Matt. 9:9). Matthew did follow Him, and he invited Jesus to dinner at his house. Like Matthew, his friends were tax collectors and "sinners," and they came to dinner and sat down with Jesus.

The term *sinner* used in this text has more than one meaning. On the one hand, it was a label that the Pharisees stuck on anyone who didn't observe the law according to their rules and regulations. On the other hand, these friends of Matthew were guilty of notorious sins. They had given up even the pretense of religion. They were people that you and I probably would rather not be associated with. They were fornicators, gamblers, swindlers, cheaters, liars, and drunks.

Jesus shocked the Pharisees by dining with such people. Offended, they asked Jesus' disciples why He associated with known sinners. They didn't ask because they truly cared for Jesus and His disciples; they just wanted to shame the Master and His followers. The Pharisees were trying to assassinate Jesus' character, for in their eyes He was guilty by association. "Doesn't He know who they are?" their words implied. "Is this any way for a proper rabbi to behave?"

Jesus responded by saying, "They that are whole have no need of the physician, but they that are sick: I came not to call the righteous, but sinners to repentance" (Mark 2:17). What a relief it is to know that the Son of God not only associates with sinners but offers to heal their sickness and cleanse them of sin! Jesus came to call sinners to repentance. Had the Pharisees recognized and acknowledged their own sin, they would have realized that they had as much need of the Savior as anyone else.

After a long day of conflict with the Pharisees, Jesus preached on the necessity of following Him (Luke 14:25–35). He concluded with this warning, "He that hath ears to hear, let him hear" (v. 35). In chapter 15, we read that the publicans and sinners pressed forward to hear what Jesus had to say. But the Pharisees and scribes continued to complain, saying, "This man receiveth sinners, and eateth with them" (vv. 1–2). Jesus then told three parables: one about a lost sheep, the next about a lost coin, and the third about a lost son. Each parable illustrates the joy of those in heaven over the good news of even one sinner who repents. Each also illustrates the sad state of those who do not recognize their need of repentance, such as the elder brother who acts like a Pharisee by refusing to go to the father's house to celebrate the restoration of the prodigal son (15:28).

The Pharisees thought they were the best of believers. They were not like the tax collectors, who betrayed fellow Jews by overcharging them with taxes to line their own pockets and those of their Roman overlords. They were not like notorious sinners, either, who wasted themselves and their goods in godless living. The Pharisees demonstrate the great danger of deceiving ourselves into thinking that we have no sin to repent of (1 John 4:8). If we think we are good, then we, like the Pharisees, will miss God's great offer of salvation to sinners. The Pharisees heeded God's warnings not to associate with sinners (Ps. 1:1; Prov. 1:10; cf. 1 Cor. 15:33), but they missed His command to teach transgressors His ways and to convert sinners to Himself (Ps. 51:13; cf. Ps. 25:8). God's plan of redemption is exclusively for sinners, even those who consider themselves morally noble and religious.

Jesus calls *all* sinners to repent. True repentance is not a nebulous response of sorrow; it requires definite actions. Repentance so transforms the mind that it results in a changed life. Repentance does not merely say "I'm sorry" (similar to what we say when we accidentally step on someone's foot). Rather, true repentance says from the heart, "I've been wrong and grieve over my sin, but now I see the truth, and I will change my ways accordingly."

The first step of repentance, according to the Heidelberg Catechism, "is heartfelt sorrow that we have provoked God by our sins." This sorrow, coupled with a deep sense of God's majesty and a profound awareness of His goodness, causes us to hate our sins more and more. This sorrow and hatred, in turn, cause us to flee from sin. True repentance also leads to "heartfelt joy in God through Christ, and with love and delight to live according to the will of God in all good works" (Heidelberg Catechism, Q. 90). Mere sorrow over sin that does not lead to changed living is a sham (2 Cor. 7:9–10).

Jesus still calls sinners—even the greatest of sinners—to join Him in His kingdom. His call does not ask us to do penance by increasing our religious duties, but to truly repent, that is, to cease from sin, turn back to the path of righteousness, and walk in new obedience to God (cf. Hosea 6:6). Those who practice true repentance know what Jesus meant when He said, "I will have mercy, and not sacrifice" (Matt. 9:13). When they, by grace, respond to that call, they will experience deep joy in union with the Friend of sinners. And nothing causes more joy in heaven than the repentance of His called ones!

17

TO DIE

Verily, verily, I say unto you, Except a corn of wheat fall into the ground and die, it abideth alone: but if it die, it bringeth forth much fruit. He that loveth his life shall lose it; and he that hateth his life in this world shall keep it unto life eternal.... Now is my soul troubled; and what shall I say? Father, save me from this hour: but for this cause came I unto this hour.

—JOHN 12:24–25, 27

Jesus was born to die. It is hard for us to grasp that truth, for we were created to live, not to die. Death is an intruder and a great enemy to life.

Yet we may also find it comforting that Jesus came to die. Hebrews 9:27 says, "It is appointed unto men once to die, but after this the judgment." We each have an appointed time to die. So did Jesus. He came to earth to die so that He, "for the suffering of death, crowned with glory and honour...by the grace of God should taste death for every man" (Heb. 2:9). As the familiar Christmas hymn points out: "Mild He lays His glory by / Born that man no more may die."

Jesus said, "For this cause came I unto this hour" (John 12:27). His appointed hour was so monumentally important in redemption that Christ referred to it as His hour.

On two earlier occasions when Jesus was threatened with physical violence, we read that He was spared because "His hour was not yet come" (John 7:30; 8:20). In our text, Jesus announced that His hour, the hour of His suffering and death, had finally come.

Consider the various human emotions Jesus revealed in talking about His hour. At first He talks about death rather positively. He says, "Except a corn of wheat fall into the ground and die, it abideth alone: but if it die, it bringeth forth much fruit." Jesus uses a simple agricultural illustration here. A single seed could produce a crop a hundred times as great as itself (Luke 8:8). But this illustration also reveals a profound spiritual reality, for Jesus is the promised "seed of the woman" (Gen. 3:15), who is about to die to produce much fruit (Gal. 3:16).

Jesus then says that to secure eternal life in the world to come, a person must be willing to part with his present life in the world. He then issued a call to follow Him, reminding us, as Dietrich Bonhoeffer said, that "Jesus bids us come and die."[1] The invitation to die will result in great fruitfulness!

But Jesus' tone changes. He says in verse 27, "Now is my soul troubled." He knows that death is evil and unnatural. In the words of Calvin, death exercises a "violent tyranny." Christ also knows that His death will be uniquely and unspeakably dreadful. He knows that in death He will bear in body and soul "the wrath of God against the sin of the whole human race" (Heidelberg Catechism, Q. 37). Death for Him will also plunge Him into the unspeakable horror of hell. In the hour of His death, Jesus will experience for the first time a terrifying alienation from His heavenly Father (Matt. 27:46).

His hour has been set from all eternity by the counsel of Father, Son, and Holy Spirit to redeem a remnant of humans for the praise of God. The minute Jesus came to earth, the countdown to His hour began. His suffering began that very moment, not at the cross. As the Heidelberg Catechism says, "He, all the time that He lived on earth, but especially at the end of His life, sustained in body and soul the wrath of God against the sins of all mankind" (Q. 37). When you find out that you need a painful surgery, the news comes as a heavy blow. But when you come to the hospital and put on a hospital gown, the long-anticipated pain of surgery and the fear of death become even more real. Then an aide comes and wheels you down the hallway toward the operating room. I wonder how many patients have had anguished second thoughts about surgery at that moment.

In our text, Jesus gives us a precious glimpse into His humanity. He approaches death as a real man. He experiences the fear of death as we do. As you reflect on your own death, remember that Jesus knows what it means to fear death. Calvin goes so far as to say, "By shrinking from death [Jesus] confesses His cowardice. Yet there is nothing in this passage that is not in perfect harmony, as every believer knows by his own experience."[2]

Even so, Jesus does not falter in His determination to fulfill His mission on earth. John offers us two reasons that is so. First, Jesus came to die. He says, "For this cause came I unto this hour" (v. 27). He also reminds Himself of His mission. In the midst of a dark battle, military leaders often rally their troops by reminding them why they have come to the battlefield and the cause for which they are prepared to make the ultimate sacrifice. Likewise, Jesus rallies His own soul, reminding Himself that He came to die for the fallen but beloved objects of God's electing grace.

Second, Jesus reminds Himself of His heart's desire to glorify God. He says, "Father, glorify thy name" (v. 28). Jesus knows that His death will bring glory to God by satisfying justice, repelling the curse against sin, defeating the devil, and securing a people zealous to praise His Father. So Jesus presses on.

Christ was born with a death sentence already hanging over him at the manger. That thought should bring us some gravity as we reflect on our Lord's advent. But it should also help us see the utter resolve of Christ to redeem His people. That determination burned within Him from the cradle to the grave. In "Christians Awake, Salute the Happy Morn," hymn writer John Byrom helps us connect the cradle with the cross: "Trace we the Babe, who hath retrieved our loss, / From His poor manger to His bitter cross."

18

TO SEEK AND SAVE
THE LOST

> *And when Jesus came to the place, he looked up, and saw him, and said unto him, Zacchaeus, make haste, and come down; for to day I must abide at thy house.… And Jesus said unto him, This day is salvation come to this house, forsomuch as he also is a son of Abraham. For the Son of man is come to seek and to save that which was lost.*
>
> —LUKE 19:5, 9–10; cf. MATTHEW 18:11

Luke 19 inspired the words to this children's song:

> Zacchaeus was a wee little man,
> And a wee little man was he.
> He climbed up in a sycamore tree
> For the Lord he wanted to see;
> And as the Savior passed that way,
> He looked up in the tree,
> And He said, "Zacchaeus, you come down!
> For I'm going to your house today."

It isn't a bad song, but it accurately records only part of the story. It also stresses the wrong problem. The great problem isn't that Zacchaeus was *small*; it is that he was *lost*. He was rich and powerful but utterly lost. He had much treasure on earth but none in heaven. He had charted a course for his life, expecting to find satisfaction in the ever-increasing possession of things. But in the process of selling His soul for money and power, he had completely lost the way to eternal life. The good news for Zacchaeus, and for us, is that Jesus came to seek and save the lost.

When Jesus said that He came to seek and save that which was lost, He was primarily talking about the lost sheep of Israel (Matt. 15:24). Zacchaeus was one of these lost sheep. He was a son of Abraham according to the flesh—that is, he was Jewish by birth. Although a child of the covenant, he had been cut out of the family line by his own unbelief and idolatry of riches. He was one of those Jews Paul describes in Romans 9:4: an Israelite "to whom pertaineth the adoption, and the glory, and the covenants, and the giving of the law, and the service of God, and the promises." He was, nonetheless, ignorant of God's righteousness, while attempting instead to establish his own righteousness (Rom. 10:3). Worse yet, he trusted not in the living God but in "uncertain riches" for security and happiness in life (1 Tim. 6:17). As a result, he was lost. Some people in the covenant community today are like Zacchaeus. They have been given so much light and so many privileges, but they are utterly lost.

But Jesus didn't come only for the lost sheep of Israel. Christ said, "Other sheep I have, which are not of this fold" (John 10:16). These other sheep are also lost. The "fold" of God represents the redeemed of God—the living church, which is united by a common profession of faith in its Shepherd, Jesus Christ. Ordinarily, people outside of this fold have no hope and no true life.

Do you remember the last time you were an outsider? If so, you know what it feels like to be lost. You live with a disquieting sense that you don't belong and that what has been given to others is denied to you. Many of God's people can remember what it is like to be without Christ, without hope, and without God in the world (Eph. 2:12). Some have lived this way in the world, while others were nurtured in the bosom of the church. Both types of people have the same sense that they are strangers to God and to grace.

Jesus came to seek these lost persons and save them. God in Christ is a seeker (Luke 15:3–6). Nineteenth-century British poet Francis Thompson affectionately refers to God as the "hound of heaven" in a poem by that name. The author recounts how he deliberately fled from God, but throughout his life he sensed he was being followed by feet that moved "with un-hurrying chase and unperturbed pace" to bring him to salvation. Without fail, God always gets His man.

When Christ came to Zacchaeus's tree, He called the little man by name. Given Zacchaeus's vocation as a tax collector, his name was probably often spoken in derision or disgust. But Jesus spoke his name with respect, enthusiasm, and purpose. No doubt to his own surprise, Zacchaeus responded to Jesus hastily and joyfully (v. 6). The Lord knew Zacchaeus by name! And, by God's grace, Zacchaeus recognized the sound of his Shepherd's voice (John 10:16)!

Zacchaeus had climbed a tree out of curiosity to see Jesus. But God was drawing him up into that tree so that Christ might find him. Christ called him down from the tree to embrace him. That day Zacchaeus came to know the life-changing experience of an anonymous poet:

> I sought the Lord, and afterward I knew
> He moved my soul to seek Him, seeking me.
> It was not I that found, O Savior true;
> No, I was found, was found of Thee.[1]

Zacchaeus could then pray with David:

> O Lord, regard me when I cry,
> In mercy hear me when I speak;
> Thou bidst me seek Thy face, and I,
> O Lord, with willing heart reply,
> Thy face, Lord, will I seek.

> —versification of Psalm 27:7–8,
> *The Psalter*, no. 73:2

The name of a church in Honesdale, Pennsylvania, is Lost and Found Bible Church. What a great reminder that Jesus came to earth to seek and save the lost.

19

TO SERVE

For even the Son of man came not to be ministered unto, but to minister, and to give his life a ransom for many.

—MARK 10:45

When was the last time you experienced genuine service? I don't mean good service at a restaurant or hotel. Even the best service we experience in such places is not true service in the biblical sense. People in the service industry are paid for their labors. Since they are often tipped for good performance, there is a direct pay-off for being friendly and helpful. Christian service has no such immediate pay-off in view. Christian service is done strictly for the benefit of others and for the glory of God.

Jesus defines true service by describing the work of a servant or slave. He says, "And whosoever of you will be the chiefest, shall be servant of all" (Mark 10:44). In Bible times, though slaves were sometimes treated as family members, they were usually regarded strictly as property. A slave was bound to another to the utter disregard of his own interests.

We are not naturally wired for that kind of service. We are like the disciples who came to Jesus asking Him to "do for us whatsoever we shall desire" (10:35). We like to "exercise lordship" over other human beings (10:42). We want to be masters, and we want to be served. Yet Jesus tells His disciples throughout the ages: "So shall it not be among you: but whosoever will be great among you, shall be your minister: and whosoever of you will be the chiefest, shall be servant of all" (10:43–44).

It's one thing for a great teacher to speak to others of humble service. But how many people who hold lofty ideals actually practice them? So that no one would think He was speaking empty rhetoric, Jesus makes this shocking statement: "For even the Son of man came not to be ministered unto, but to minister, and to give his life a ransom for many" (10:45). Christ served by giving His time, sometimes ministering until the late hours of the evening (Mark 6:35). He served the ungrateful (Luke 17:14–18), the unpopular (Matt. 11:19), and the untouchable (Mark 1:40–42). When He washed the feet of His disciples, He stooped beneath the status of most household servants (John 13:3–17), since foot washing was the work of the lowest rank. Jesus became like a slave so that we might be free in Him.

One of the great paradoxes in the Bible is that because of the work of Christ, believers are both slaves and sons. Many in the New Testament church actually were slaves, so Paul offers a lesson to both slaves and freemen in the church: "For he that is called in the Lord, being a servant, is the Lord's freeman: likewise also he that is called, being free, is Christ's servant" (1 Cor. 7:22). Paul identifies himself both as a servant of God (Titus 1:1) and, through Christ, "no more a servant, but a son" (Gal. 4:7). To be both a slave and a son is a reflection of the person of Jesus Christ. Though Christ was a Son, He learned obedience as the Suffering

Servant of the Lord (Heb. 5:8, cf. Isa. 53). His work was greatest when it seemed the lowest. Though He collapsed in the dust carrying the cross for our salvation, He was and is always the King of kings.

If you look around for examples of humble service, you won't find many. As William Hendriksen says, "Jesus is saying that in the kingdom over which he reigns, greatness is obtained by pursuing a course of action which is the exact opposite of that which is followed in the unbelieving world."[1] Jesus lived among His disciples as an example for us all. After washing His disciples' feet, He said, "For I have given you an example, that ye should do as I have done to you. Verily, verily, I say unto you, The servant is not greater than his lord; neither he that is sent greater than he that sent him" (John 13:15–16).

How could you serve others this week as an example of Christ? How could you stoop beneath your station in life to bless someone? These are important questions, so take them seriously. But make sure that as you wrestle with these questions your thoughts stay rooted in this grand reality: "Even the Son of man came not to be ministered unto, but to minister."

TO BRING PEACE

*For he is our peace, who hath made both one, and hath bro-
ken down the middle wall of partition between us; having
abolished in his flesh the enmity, even the law of commandments contained in ordinances; for to make in himself of
twain one new man, so making peace; and that he might
reconcile both unto God in one body by the cross, having
slain the enmity thereby: and came and preached peace to you
which were afar off, and to them that were nigh. For through
him we both have access by one Spirit unto the Father.*
—EPHESIANS 2:14–18; cf. ACTS 10:36

When we hear the word *peace,* we may think about the
so-called peace movement in the 1960s. In opposition to
military conflict abroad and perceived societal oppression at
home, "peace" became a popular slogan in the hippie movement. The irony was that the movement could not produce
what it promised. Even communes that were founded on
peaceful principles such as equality and sharing nearly all fell
apart due to internal and external conflict.[1] No man-made
community, however lofty its ideals, will ever secure peace.
We would realize this if we only asked the right questions.

Jesus' half-brother James asked the right questions:
"From whence come wars and fightings among you? come

they not hence, even of your lusts that war in your members? Ye lust, and have not: ye kill, and desire to have, and cannot obtain: ye fight and war, yet ye have not, because ye ask not" (James 4:1–2). Rivers of peace will never flow from the polluted spring of the unregenerate human heart. One reason Jesus came to earth was to extend "peace…like a river" to His church (Isa. 66:12).

In Ephesians 2, Paul makes three amazing statements about Jesus and peace. First he says that Jesus came preaching peace (v. 17; cf. John 14:27). The angelic announcement of Jesus' birth was "peace on earth" (Luke 2:14). Likewise, Jesus' message that "the kingdom of God is at hand: repent ye, and believe the gospel" is a message of peace (Mark 1:15). To understand this, picture a vast army rising against an inferior force. The smaller army has no chance of success. But just before the inevitable attack, an ambassador from the greater army brings this message: "Our king promises to make peace with you if only you will concede defeat and pledge loyalty to his service." What a relief!

This is Jesus' main message as well. Jesus even proclaimed peace to the wind-tossed sea, saying, "Peace, be still" (Mark 4:39). Paul reflected Jesus' ministry when he said, "We pray you in Christ's stead, be ye reconciled to God" (2 Cor. 5:20). Wars will cease and peace will reign on earth only when sinful mankind is finally reconciled to God through Jesus Christ.

Second, Paul says that Christ has secured peace between Jew and Gentile (Eph. 2:14). It is wearying to think about the peace talks in the Middle East that have been going on for decades. How much energy and time have been poured into this peace process, which as yet has yielded only meager results? But Jesus actually secured peace. He says, "Peace I leave with you, my peace I give unto you: not as the world giveth, give I unto you. Let not your heart be troubled, neither let it be afraid" (John 14:27). When Christ died, He wiped out "the handwriting of ordinances that was against us, which was contrary to us, and took it out of the way, nailing it to his cross" (Col. 2:14). Believers who fear the wrath of God because of their sins need to remember that God has made permanent peace between Himself and elect sinners who repent and believe in His Son, who bore God's anger for them. Because of the peace Christ has secured for believers, God says, "If it be possible, as much as lieth in you, live peaceably with all men" (Rom. 12:18). In large letters the cross has written peace on our hearts.

Third, Paul says that Jesus is our peace (Eph. 2:14). In the Old Testament Jesus is called the Prince of Peace. The prophet Isaiah adds, "Of the increase of his government and peace there shall be no end (Isa. 9:7). What is peace? From the Greek word *eirene,* we get the word *irenic,* which refers to peace. The Hebrew word for peace is *shalom.* These words denote not only cessation of strife and the calm that follows, but also a wholeness and completeness that are found in Christ alone (Col. 2:10). These terms speak of the peace that believers have with God and also of the peace of God that dwells in their minds and hearts. As the saying goes, "No Jesus, no peace. Know Jesus, know peace." Only those who are under the reign of the Prince of Peace truly know "the peace...which passeth all understanding" (Phil. 4:7).

The unbeliever needs to grasp the dreadful truth declared by the Lord in Isaiah 48:22: "There is no peace, saith the LORD, unto the wicked." After James concludes his scathing critique of man's warmongering heart he says bluntly, "Ye have not, because ye ask not. Ye ask, and receive not, because ye ask amiss, that ye may consume it upon your lusts" (James 4:2–3). Those who long for peace should ask of God "that giveth to all men liberally" (James 1:5), praying, "Lord, make peace between Thee and me by the blood of Christ."

Matthew Henry summed up the matter by saying, "Sin breeds a quarrel between God and man. Christ came to take up that quarrel and bring it to an end."[2] Those who have "peace with God through our Lord Jesus Christ" (Rom. 5:1) cherish the promise that one day He will reign over the world as the Prince of Peace:

> O God, be Thy Anointed Son
> With truth and righteousness endowed,
> That justice may on earth be done,
> The meek protected from the proud.
>
> The just shall flourish in His day,
> And ever more shall peace extend;
> From sea to sea shall be His sway,
> And to the earth's remotest end.
>
> —versification of Psalm 72:1–2, 7–8,
> *The Psalter*, no. 198:1, 5

TO BRING A SWORD

Think not that I am come to send peace on earth: I came not to send peace, but a sword.

— MATTHEW 10:34; cf. LUKE 12:51–53

Every New Testament writer uses the word *peace* in every New Testament book except 1 John. Zechariah prophesied that Jesus would come to "guide our feet into the way of peace," and, at Jesus' birth, the angels say, "On earth peace, good will toward men" (Luke 1:79; 2:14). Peace is the pervasive theme of Jesus' ministry. So how can Jesus say in Matthew 10:34, "Think not that I am come to send peace on earth: I came not to send peace, but a sword"?

First, consider the context of Matthew 10. Jesus is addressing His disciples before sending them out "as sheep in the midst of wolves" (v. 16). Jesus does not want them to be naïve about the people to whom they are sent. He warns them not to think that everyone will welcome them when they hear that they are sent from Him, for they will not. Jesus also says that some households will not be worthy of the message of peace that the disciples bring. When the disciples encounter such households they are to let their salutation of peace "return to them" (v. 13); that is, they are not to use the customary words of benediction "peace be with you" both to greet and to say farewell to these ungrateful people.

Jesus says the one who hears His call to discipleship should recognize it as the declaration of a king going to make war against a rival ruler. Before he does so, he counts the costs (Luke 14:25–33). Christ braces His disciples by warning them about what they will face. He speaks as a warrior, saying, "I bring a sword!" The peace of God is the prize of a great war! Christ has entered the house of the strong man, Satan, and plundered his goods, having first bound the strong man, says Matthew 12:29. The disciples also are to bring the sword of the Spirit, the Word of God (Eph. 6:17). Clad with the armor of God, disciples need not fear their enemies (Matt. 10:26).

Second, Jesus says that the message of the kingdom of heaven will evoke two responses. Some who hear the message will confess Christ before others, and Jesus will confess these before His Father in heaven. Others will deny Jesus before men, and Christ will deny these before His Father in heaven (Matt. 10:32–33). Christ says that He comes to draw a line in the sand: "He that is not with me is against me; and he that gathereth not with me scattereth abroad" (Matt. 12:30). These are fighting words!

Finally, Jesus says, the gospel is sure to bring divisions. He says, "For I am come to set a man at variance against his father, and the daughter against her mother, and the daughter in law against her mother in law. And a man's foes shall be they of his own household" (Matt. 10:35–36). As J. C. Ryle explains, "So long as someone is resolved to keep his sins; and another desirous to give them up, the result of the preaching of the Gospel must needs be division. For that the Gospel is not to blame, but the heart of man."[1] Micah 7, from which Jesus quotes, is a rallying cry to trust only in the Lord, not in friends or family members, when it comes to life-and-death spiritual issues. Such faith will cut like a sword.

Christ brings a sword because He confronts us with a choice: "Love me first over everything else that is dear, or you are not worthy of Me. Put your selfish desires to death daily, or you are not worthy of Me. Lose your life, and you will find it." As Ryle says, "Though Christianity holds out a crown in the end, it brings also a cross in the way."[2] Those who put peace with their fellow men before loyalty to Christ are not worthy of Him.

A sword divides. On one side of Christ's sword is misery and death. On the other side is joy and life. On which side of Christ's sword do you stand today?

22

TO BIND UP
BROKEN HEARTS

The Spirit of the Lord GOD is upon me; because the LORD hath anointed me to preach good tidings unto the meek; he hath sent me to bind up the brokenhearted, to proclaim liberty to the captives, and the opening of the prison to them that are bound; to proclaim the acceptable year of the LORD, and the day of vengeance of our God; to comfort all that mourn; to appoint unto them that mourn in Zion, to give unto them beauty for ashes, the oil of joy for mourning, the garment of praise for the spirit of heaviness; that they might be called trees of righteousness, the planting of the LORD, that he might be glorified.

—ISAIAH 61:1–3

The nineteenth-century British preacher Alexander Maclaren said, "No man will ever do much for the world whose ears have not been opened to hear its sad music."[1] As the incarnate Son of God, Jesus heard the world's sad music. Touched "with the feeling of our infirmities" (Heb. 4:14), the Man of Sorrows experienced firsthand that the world is filled with broken hearts. That is why Jesus' announcement that He came to fulfill Isaiah 61 is music to the ears of the brokenhearted.

Every child of God has felt his soul cleave to the dust and melt for heaviness (Ps. 119:25, 28). Circumstances can overwhelm us with hopelessness. Life in a sinful world weighs heavily on our hearts. On top of this sorrow is the pain that comes from persecution by the ungodly. The psalmist testifies of this: "My tears have been my meat day and night, while they continually say unto me, Where is thy God?" (Ps. 42:3). Thankfully, Christ has come to heal all the brokenness of believers' hearts. Jesus' coming and His ministry in word and deed point to a day when all things will be made right, when "God shall wipe away all tears" from the eyes of His redeemed people. As Revelation 21:4 says, "There shall be no more death, neither sorrow, nor crying, neither shall there be any more pain: for the former things are passed away."

Jesus' promise to bind up the brokenhearted is of particular comfort to God's children as they grieve over their sins. A broken heart deplores its uncleanness and asks the Lord to cleanse it (Ps. 51:10). For example, after his shameful moral lapse, David's heart was broken. He knew he had sinned not only against Bathsheba and Uriah but also against the Lord. At least fifteen times in Psalm 51 he uses words specifying the nature of his sin as "transgressions" (vv. 1, 3, 13); "iniquity" (vv. 2, 5, 9); "sin" (vv. 2–5, 9, 13); "evil" (v. 4); and "bloodguiltiness" (v. 14).

David's heart was broken by the sense of his sin. He felt as if God had broken his very bones (v. 8). Because of his guilt, God's hand was heavy upon him; he felt the kind of dehydration and thirst associated with such guilt and said, "My moisture is turned into the drought of summer" (Ps. 32:4). Still, David knew that God would heal his heart. He thus wrote, "The sacrifices of God are a broken spirit: a

broken and contrite heart, O God, thou wilt not despise"
(Ps. 51:17).

The Hebrew version of Isaiah 61:1 literally says that
Christ "bandages" the brokenhearted. What a beautiful picture this is of Christ healing the broken in heart and binding
up their wounds (Ps. 147:3; cf. Luke 10:34). His gentle
touch as a physician of souls was described in prophecy: "A
bruised reed shall he not break, and smoking flax shall he
not quench" (Isa. 42:3; cf. Matt. 12:20).

This imagery of Jesus' tender care is particularly striking
in light of Scripture's portrayal of Him as a warrior king.
Psalm 2 says that the Messiah will govern the nations with
the severity of divine justice. Christ will "break them with a
rod of iron" and "dash them in pieces like a potter's vessel"
(v. 9). The difference lies in one's heart response to Christ's
government. In Psalm 2 the nations resist the rule of Christ.
In Isaiah 42 the Gentiles submit to Him and eagerly wait for
His law. Christ is both a strong ruler and a gentle healer. To
the brokenhearted, He is gentle; to those who oppose Him,
He is a crushing warrior.

In Christ the gentleness and might of God is revealed.
A loving husband will gently caress his wife when she has
had a rough day. But he is ready to fight anyone who harms
her. Knowing that we have such a husband in Christ, let us
take the posture of a bruised reed that bends down toward
the ground as if paying homage. "Be afflicted, and mourn,
and weep.... Humble yourselves in the sight of the Lord,
and he shall lift you up" (James 4:9–10). Then we can sing
with David:

Thy free salvation is my shield,
My sure defense in every strait;
Thy hand upholds me, lest I yield;
Thy gentleness has made me great.

—versification of Psalm 18:35,
The Psalter, no. 35:6

23

TO GIVE US THE
SPIRIT OF ADOPTION

And I will pray the Father, and he shall give you another Comforter, that he may abide with you forever; even the Spirit of truth.

—JOHN 14:16–17

And because ye are sons, God hath sent forth the Spirit of his Son into your hearts, crying, Abba, Father.

—GALATIANS 4:6

Our hearts are wonderfully warmed when we read the answer to question 26 in the Heidelberg Catechism. To the question "What believest thou when thou sayest, 'I believe in God the Father, Almighty, Maker of heaven and earth?'" comes in part the answer: "That the eternal Father of our Lord Jesus Christ (who out of nothing made heaven and earth, with all that is in them, who likewise upholds and governs them by His eternal counsel and providence), is for the sake of Christ His Son, my God and Father."

Those words remind us of the priority of the Father-Son relationship over that of the Creator-creature relationship. In other words, before God is the almighty Creator through Christ by the Spirit, He is the eternal Father of the Son, in union and communion with the Holy Spirit.

The love of the Father for the Son is extended to those chosen human beings for whom the Son lays down His life. They are granted access into the life, love, unity, and glory of the Godhead, to the extent that such a thing is possible for mere finite creatures. Jesus alludes to this in His High Priestly Prayer:

> [I pray] that they all may be one; as thou, Father, art in me, and I in thee, that they also may be one in us: that the world may believe that thou hast sent me. And the glory which thou gavest me I have given them; that they may be one, even as we are one: I in them, and thou in me, that they may be made perfect in one; and that the world may know that thou hast sent me, and hast loved them, as thou hast loved me (John 17:21–23).

This is why Jesus taught His disciples in the Lord's Prayer to begin by addressing God as "Our Father" (Matt. 6:9). As the Heidelberg Catechism says so beautifully, Christ does so to "excite in us a childlike reverence for and confidence in God, which are the foundation of our prayer, namely that God is become our Father in Christ" (Q. 120).

This is also why God gives us the Holy Spirit as the Spirit of adoption or sonship. Paul writes in his epistle to the Galatians: "And because ye are sons, God hath sent forth the Spirit of his Son into your hearts, crying, Abba, Father" (Gal. 4:6). He writes something similar to the saints in Rome: "Ye have received the Spirit of adoption, whereby we cry, Abba, Father. The Spirit itself beareth witness with our spirit, that we are the children of God" (Rom. 8:15–16).

This is the Spirit that the Lord Jesus Christ poured out on the day of Pentecost. On that day, Peter identified the sound "as of a mighty, rushing wind," the cloven tongues as of fire, and the speaking in different languages as signs of Christ's outpouring of the Holy Spirit. He says, "Therefore being by the right hand of God exalted, and having received of the Father the promise of the Holy Ghost, he hath shed forth this, which ye now see and hear" (Acts 2:33). He adds: "Therefore let all the house of Israel know assuredly, that God hath made the same Jesus, whom ye have crucified, both Lord and Christ" (Acts 2:36). The multitude of listeners were pricked in their hearts and asked him and the other apostles what they should do to be saved. Peter answers: "Repent, and be baptized every one of you in the name of Jesus Christ for the remission of sins, and ye shall receive the gift of the Holy Ghost. For the promise is unto you, and to your children, and to all that are afar off, even as many as the LORD our God shall call" (Acts 2:38–39).

Christ came to earth so that through the Holy Spirit we could share in the eternal relationship between God the Father and God the Son. He came to earth so that we could participate in all the honor, happiness, and privileges that are His as the beloved Son of God the Father. The Father wills that His Son should be the head of a large household—a family or band of brothers (Heb. 2:11–12; 3:6). This adoption into the family of God is more than legal status. As we learn from Christ's prayer, it is the most intimate and loving union and communion, which is nothing less than what is between the Father and the Son. It also shines with the very glory of God. Such privileges are held out to all who believe in the Son. As the psalm says:

When the Lord shall count the nations,
Sons and daughters He shall see,
Born to endless life in Zion,
And their joyful song shall be,
"Blessed Zion, all our fountains are in thee."

—versification of Psalm 87:6–7,
The Psalter, no. 238:3

24

TO MAKE US PARTAKERS
OF THE DIVINE NATURE

Whereby are given unto us exceeding great and precious promises: that by these ye might be partakers of the divine nature, having escaped the corruption that is in the world through lust.

—2 PETER 1:4

Why did Christ come to earth? Why did He have a human nature? The answer to such questions is, according to the Heidelberg Catechism, that "Christ needed to have a human nature because, since human beings sinned, a human being needs to pay for sin" (Q. 16). This answer is clearly taught in Scripture in passages like this one: "For since by man came death, by man came also the resurrection of the dead (1 Cor. 15:21; cf. Rom. 5:18). Christ, the eternal Word, was made flesh so that He could offer Himself as the atoning sacrifice for His people to make them right with God.

But lest we think that Christ's coming in the flesh affects only our standing with God, the apostle Peter introduces to us the astonishing reality that we have also been given the privilege of becoming "partakers of the divine nature" (2 Peter 1:4). Reflecting on our hopeless condition and the necessity of the incarnation, Calvin observed, "The situation would surely have been hopeless had the very majesty of God not descended to us, since it was not in our power to ascend to Him. Hence, it was necessary for the Son of God to become for us, 'Immanuel, that is God with us'...and in such a way that His divinity and our human nature might by mutual connection grow together."[1] Accordingly, Calvin continued, the Son of God became the Son of man "to impart what was His to us, and to make what was His by nature ours by grace"[2] so that He "might join us to God."[3] This joining together occurs "by the secret power of His Spirit."[4]

The secret power of the Spirit of Christ joins us to the human nature of Christ when we are engrafted into Him through faith and begin to live in Him. According to Calvin, "The flesh of Christ is like a rich and inexhaustible fountain that pours into us the life springing forth from the Godhead itself."[5] It is "the channel" by which the divine life flows into us.[6]

This divine life is twofold. First, it is the incorruptible, glorious, spiritual life that God has promised us. Because our souls are joined to Christ, we know that one day our vile bodies will be transformed into the likeness of the glorious body of the risen Christ (Phil. 3:21). Our resurrected bodies will then never get tired, fall sick, decay, or die (Rev. 21:1–4). We will have immortal bodies just like that of the risen Lord Jesus Christ. Jesus' immortal, glorified, human flesh is the channel through which we will receive the gift of physical incorruptibility or immortality. This promise will be fulfilled on the glorious day of our resurrection.

Second, this divine life is the incorruptible, glorious, spiritual life of righteousness and holiness, which God has promised us and to which He has called us today. After Peter writes about the glorious privilege of becoming partakers of the divine nature, he continues: "And beside this, giving all diligence, add to your faith virtue; and to virtue knowledge; and to knowledge temperance; and to temperance patience; and to patience godliness; and to godliness brotherly kindness; and to brotherly kindness charity" (2 Peter 1:5–7). Those are incorruptible virtues or spiritual graces that were lived out and embodied for us in the righteous and holy human life of the Lord Jesus Christ. What He has done for us He also works in us through His Holy Spirit as we abide in Christ through faith. When this happens, we receive out of the fullness of Christ's glorified, human nature "grace for grace" (John 1:16).

Until He returns, Christ has appointed the celebration of the Lord's Supper as a means of experiencing this mystery of the believer's union with Him. As Calvin said, the supper is "a mystery of Christ's secret union with the devout which is by nature incomprehensible. In the supper believers ascend into heaven where they commune with the glorified Christ."[7] This promise of sharing in the divine nature is only partly fulfilled today. But in the new heavens and the new earth it will be fulfilled to perfection, when as perfected spirits inhabiting glorified bodies, we shall live forever in the presence of our Lord.

TO REIGN AS KING

For unto us a child is born, unto us a son is given: and the government shall be upon his shoulder: and his name shall be called Wonderful, Counsellor, The mighty God, The everlasting Father, The Prince of Peace. Of the increase of his government and peace there shall be no end, upon the throne of David, and upon his kingdom, to order it, and to establish it with judgment and with justice from henceforth even for ever. The zeal of the LORD of hosts will perform this.

—ISAIAH 9:6–7

One of the great themes of the Bible is that God is "the King of all the earth" (Ps. 47:7). The first song of praise in Scripture declares, "The LORD shall reign forever and ever" (Ex. 15:18). The believer cries out to "my King, and my God," who hears and answers such prayers because He is "the King of glory" and "mighty in battle" (Pss. 5:2; 24:8). At the close of the Bible, Revelation depicts a great crowd of believers who shout, "Alleluia: for the Lord God omnipotent reigneth" (Rev. 19:6).

Another great theme of the Bible is that God appoints a human king to rule His people in His name. From the time of God's covenant with Abraham (Gen. 17:6) to His covenant with David (2 Sam. 7:12), God promised to give His people a king to rule over them. Even after Babylon conquered Jerusalem and carried her people into exile, God still held forth the promise to raise up a shepherd king in the line of David: "And I will set up one shepherd over them, and he shall feed them, even my servant David; he shall feed them, and he shall be their shepherd" (Ezek. 34:23).

Ultimately, God is king, but this king also promises to send a human king to rule in His name. Isaiah 9:6–7 declares that both of these great themes will come together in one person. This king is human, "for unto us a child is born." He has a human mother (Gal. 4:4). He arrives in the frailty of an infant. He has a human ancestry, a family tree that goes back to David, so that He has the right to sit "upon the throne of David." Yet God is still "the God of David," and His covenant stands firm (Isa. 38:5; 55:3).

We need a human king. If God ruled us directly, it would overwhelm us. Even the seraphim, which are flames of pure spiritual fire, must cover their faces before His presence (Isa. 6:2). We need a shepherd who will walk with us in the valley of the shadow of death and carry us close to His heart (Ps. 23:1–4; Isa. 40:11). Our king must have human hands to wipe tears from our eyes and a human soul to empathize with our grief. That king is Jesus.

This same king, however, is also God. With words and phrases that sparkle like diamonds, Isaiah discloses His divine attributes: "wonderful," "mighty," "everlasting," "of the increase of his government there shall be no end." He is also "the mighty God." No lower-case "god" will suffice, for Isaiah makes it clear that "the mighty God" is "the LORD, the Holy One of Israel" (Isa. 10:20–21). This king is Jehovah!

Just as we need a human king, we also need a divine king. We must have a king with supernatural wisdom to lead us out of the mess we have created by our sins. Jesus is the "wonderful counselor," having the very wisdom of the Lord God (Isa. 28:29). We need a king with infinite power to overcome sin, death, Satan, and hell. Jesus is the "mighty God," whose voice alone is a glorious weapon with which He slays His enemies (Isa. 11:4).

We also need a king who will love us forever, through all the ups and downs of our imperfect obedience. Jesus is the "everlasting father" to His people. He is full of compassion for stumbling saints. He is not God the Father, but, we may still say of Christ, "Like as a father pitieth his children, so the LORD pitieth them that fear him" (Ps. 103:13). And we must have a king who can restore true peace and harmony to our lives. Jesus is thus "the Prince of Peace," whose "peaceable kingdom" has no end. He does not bring a peace that compromises with sin, but a peace that conquers sin "with judgment and with justice" (Isa. 9:7).

Christ is King, the God-man given for us and to us. The zeal of God for His own glory guarantees that Christ's kingdom cannot fail. If you submit to Him, then one day your "eyes shall see the king in his beauty" (Isa. 33:17). What a glorious hope that is!

> His wide dominion shall extend
> From sea to utmost sea,
> And unto earth's remotest bounds
> His peaceful rule shall be.
>
> The tribes that in the desert dwell
> Shall bow before His throne;
> His enemies shall be subdued
> And He shall rule alone.
>
> —versification of Psalm 72:8–9,
> *The Psalter*, no. 194:1–2

TO RESTORE HUMAN NATURE TO HOLINESS

And the angel answered and said unto her, The Holy Ghost shall come upon thee, and the power of the Highest shall overshadow thee: therefore also that holy thing which shall be born of thee shall be called the Son of God.

—LUKE 1:35

It's a lot easier to fall into a mud puddle than it is to get the stains out of your clothes. Imagine trying to wash those dirty clothes by scrubbing them with muddy hands. How effective would that be? When man fell into sin, he fell into a pit of spiritual filth. Now all of our best effort to cleanse ourselves with muddy hands just makes things worse. Washing souls requires something clean to start with.

Job asked, "Who can bring a clean thing out of an unclean?" (14:4). Sin is so engrained in our nature that we can no sooner change the melanin that colors our skin than purge the evil that poisons our hearts (Jer. 13:23). Dark skin is beautiful (Song 1:5), but souls defiled by sin are not.

Many people are quite satisfied with a religion of external rules and ceremonies because they have a superficial view of sin. Perhaps they have fairly loose rules, such as a minimum requirement to attend public worship now and then. Or maybe they have stiff and complex rules consisting of behaviors almost as intricate as a Japanese tea ceremony. Either way, changes in behavior cannot purify the heart, for it is the seat of our corruption. Christ said, "Either make the tree good, and his fruit good; or else make the tree corrupt, and his fruit corrupt: for the tree is known by his fruit" (Matt. 12:33).

Jesus came to become the root of a whole new tree. He is also the vine and we are the branches (John 15:5). He is the head, and we are the members of His body, the church (Eph. 4:15–16). He did not come to merely teach us the way; He blazed the trail as the author and finisher of our faith. Now we can run the race set before us by looking unto Him by the faith He works in our hearts. We are sanctified because we are Christ's brothers, made one with Him, the one who sanctifies (Heb. 2:10–11; 12:1–2).

That is why the virgin birth of Christ is so important. Some people have stumbled at this miracle, finding it impossible to believe, because babies are ordinarily conceived by the union of a father and mother. However, if God has the power to create the universe out of nothing and to make the human race out of the dust of the earth, then a virgin birth is child's play to Him. As the angel said to Mary, "With God nothing shall be impossible" (Luke 1:37).

But God's purpose in the virgin birth was not just to show His power to do the impossible. The angel explained to Mary how she would conceive a child without a human partner: "The Holy Ghost shall come upon thee, and the power of the Highest shall overshadow thee: therefore also that holy thing which shall be born of thee shall be called the Son of God" (Luke 1:35).

The Holy Spirit furnished the eternal Son of God with a human nature from the flesh and blood of His virgin mother in such a way that Christ was holy, blameless, undefiled, and free from sin from the moment of His conception. For a moment, God dammed up the flood of wickedness pouring through the line of Adam's race, and not a drop of contaminated water entered Jesus' soul.

Just as Sarah miraculously conceived Isaac, the first child of the promise, so Mary also supernaturally conceived the first child of the new creation. God's glory overshadowed the tabernacle in Moses' day (Ex. 40:35), but in Christ the divine glory would "overshadow" human nature to restore it as the temple of the living God. The firstborn son of Mary was holy because His very conception was the work of the Holy Spirit.

In that miraculous birth there is hope for a race defiled by sin. What we cannot do for ourselves is wrought in us by the power of God. We too can be made holy by the Holy Spirit, who unites us with the holy Son of God. Our destiny is to be conformed to His image in righteousness and holiness (Rom. 8:29). So Christ restores holiness in the unholy, and beauty to those defaced by sin.

TO BE A MERCIFUL AND
FAITHFUL HIGH PRIEST

Wherefore in all things it behoved him to be made like unto his brethren, that he might be a merciful and faithful high priest in things pertaining to God, to make reconciliation for the sins of the people. For in that he himself hath suffered being tempted, he is able to succour them that are tempted.

—HEBREWS 2:17–18

God is offended by sin. He is not petty in this, like some kind of cosmic control freak. He hates sin for its infinite ugliness. His burning wrath against sin is the other side of His holy love of righteousness (Ps. 11:5–7). God is indeed good, but this is bad news for us, for we all sin (1 Kings 8:46). We all deserve to hear the Lord say, with justice burning in His eyes, "Depart from me, ye cursed, into everlasting fire" (Matt. 25:41).

How can we live with such a holy God, much less draw near to Him in worship? That was precisely the problem that ancient Israel faced. God opened the way for man to interact with Him by instituting sacrifices for sin and appointing the priesthood. He instituted a system of rituals by which Aaron and his sons drew near to Him and offered sacrifices for the people (Ex. 28–29). They brought the blood of sacrifices and sin offerings into God's holy presence to atone for the sins of the people and to intercede for God's forgiveness and blessing upon Israel.

God also built into the whole system a profound sense of inadequacy. If the priests did not follow His instructions, they died (Lev. 10:1–3). The sacrifices were animals, which could hardly pay the price once and for all for human sins. Because they couldn't, the sacrifices had to be offered again and again. What's more, the people themselves could not enter into God's most holy presence but had to worship outside, in the outer court of the tabernacle. The whole system was just a shadow pointing to a coming reality (Heb. 9:7–8; 10:1–4).

The true priesthood arrived in Christ. In Hebrews 2:17–18, the Holy Spirit tells us that the Son of God became a man because He had to become "in all things…like unto his brethren." Christ's "brethren" are the people whom He came to save, the chosen spiritual seed of the covenant (Heb. 2:16), who in due time would be sanctified by His priestly ministry (Heb. 2:11).

There are two reasons Christ had to become human to be a merciful and faithful high priest. First, a high priest had to make reconciliation for the sins of the people. As a human high priest, Christ propitiated, or quenched, the anger of God, so that He was free to forgive sinners (Ps. 78:38). This high priest offered Himself as a sacrifice according to the will of His Father, to make us holy once and for all in God's sight (Heb. 10:10–14).

Because He saved us by the offering of His body, Christ had to become flesh and blood like us in every way except for our sin (Heb. 2:14; 4:15). What amazing love He has for us! Christ as God is an infinite and immortal spirit, yet He took a human head so it could be struck, crowned with thorns, and beaten with a reed. He took a human body so it could be ripped open with a Roman scourge. He took human arms and legs so they could be stretched out on the cross, and human hands so that they could be nailed to its wood. He took a human soul so He could feel the unspeakable pain of His Father forsaking Him in the darkness. He took our very nature so that He could bleed and die for the sins that we committed. As John 15:13 says, "Greater love hath no man than this."

Second, a high priest must intercede for God's grace to help "them that are tempted" (Heb. 2:18). The high priest Aaron entered the most holy place with blood and sweet incense, bearing on his shoulder and breastplate the names of the tribes of Israel, but Jesus Christ ascended into heaven itself with the merit of His sufferings and obedience, bearing our names in His heart, there to intercede for us.

This priest intercedes for us with a heart of tender compassion because "he himself hath suffered being tempted." He is "touched with the feeling of our infirmities" (Heb. 4:15). When He sees our sinful failings, our stumbling obedience, and our inept, inarticulate prayers, His heart is moved with love. He remembers His own struggles, prayers, and tears (Heb. 5:9).

Therefore, let us draw near to God with full assurance, trusting in our only High Priest in order that our hearts may be strengthened with the grace that Jesus Christ knows we need for today.

TO BE THE SECOND
AND GREATER ADAM

Nevertheless death reigned from Adam to Moses, even over them that had not sinned after the similitude of Adam's transgression, who is the figure of him that was to come. But not as the offence, so also is the free gift. For if through the offence of one many be dead, much more the grace of God, and the gift by grace, which is by one man, Jesus Christ, hath abounded unto many.
— ROMANS 5:14–15

"In Adam's fall we sinned all," says the *New England Primer,* the basic textbook by which thousands of children once learned to read in America. Though its words are foreign to many people today, the book still reflects the biblical truth stated by Paul: "Wherefore, as by one man sin entered into the world, and death by sin; and so death passed upon all men, for that all have sinned" (Rom. 5:12).

Adam's sin was not just a bad example; by him sin entered into the world. Immediately after the fall in the book of Genesis, we read of defective worship, brother murdering brother, polygamy, and cries for vengeance (Gen. 4). Not many generations later, God surveyed mankind and grimly concluded that "every imagination of the thoughts of his heart was only evil continually" (Gen. 6:5).

Not only did sin enter and reign over mankind through Adam, but "condemnation" also fell upon "all men" by "the offence of one" (Rom. 5:18). The entire race was damned because of Adam's sin. We are all guilty in him and thus abide under the wrath of God.

Adam was not only our natural father, but he was also our head, or representative, in the covenant of God. Though Eve was with him, Adam alone received the commandment from God not to eat of the tree and the threat of death upon disobedience (Gen. 2:15–17). As king of the world, his disobedience not only brought death to himself but also accursed disorder to the earth (Gen. 3:17).

Adam's sin also brought death to his descendants (Gen. 5; Rom. 5:12, 17). For this reason Paul observed that death strikes down even those who have not yet consciously rebelled against God's law as Adam did (Rom. 5:14). How horrific the guilt of Adam's sin was that its generational tentacles seize even our little children!

In the darkness of Adam's fall, however, there was a light of hope, for Adam was "the figure of him that was to come," that is, Jesus Christ. Adam was a model, a prototype as it were, of the coming Savior. Just as Adam fell by the temptations of the serpent, so God promised that the "seed of the woman" would come and crush Satan's head (Gen. 3:15). Luke's gospel announces that the Son of God has come and traces His genealogy back to "Adam, which was the son of God" (3:22, 38). Christ overcame all the devil's temptations (Luke 4:1–13). In doing so, Jesus Christ became our new Adam who stood upright and firm, whereas the first Adam fell.

Christ is not just a good example to imitate but is the representative of His people in their legal and covenantal status before God. Adam's disobedience brought condemnation so that all men were counted as sinners, but Christ's obedience brought justification so that His people are now counted as righteous (Rom. 5:16, 19). Believers are His "seed" (Ps. 22:30), and God is pleased to justify them because their spiritual father, God's "righteous servant," bore all their iniquities (Isa. 53:10–11).

How blessed it is to be in union with Christ! He is not just the second Adam, but the ultimate Adam whose work will never be undone or replaced (1 Cor. 15:45). His righteous life, accursed death, and victorious resurrection give life to all in Him—spiritual life today and resurrection life at His coming again in glory (Eph. 2:4–7; 1 Cor. 15:22–23).

Whenever we taste the bitterness of living in a world cursed because of the first Adam's sin, let us savor the sweetness of the last Adam's obedience. Whether we feel the pain caused by natural evils like cancer, hurricanes, and birth defects, or moral evils like racism, governmental tyranny, and selfish greed, let us anchor our hope in the promise of a coming day when the entire curse will be removed and there shall be "new heavens and a new earth, wherein dwelleth righteousness" (2 Peter 3:13).

Let us exult, rejoice, and boast in the last Adam. Christ's work does not merely cancel Adam's sin. No, as Paul says, Christ has accomplished a superabundance of grace that goes above and beyond what sin destroyed (Rom. 5:15, 20). We shall not merely escape death and hell but "reign in life" through Him (Rom. 5:17). We shall be kings and priests in a new world of which Adam scarcely dreamed (Rev. 1:5–6; 5:9–10; 22:3–5).

TO SATISFY OUR
DEEPEST THIRST

*Whosoever drinketh of this water shall thirst again: but who-
soever drinketh of the water that I shall give him shall never
thirst; but the water that I shall give him shall be in him a
well of water springing up into everlasting life.*

—JOHN 4:13–14

When the disciples walked into Sychar, leaving Jesus sitting
by Jacob's well, little did they know that He was about to
keep a divine appointment. At noon (not the normal time
to draw water), a Samaritan woman came to the well with
her water jar. Shortly afterward she was back in town, water
pot forgotten, as she excitedly told everyone she met about
Christ. Two days later the Samaritans declared, "This is
indeed the Christ, the Saviour of the world" (John 4:42).

What moved the Samaritans, bitter enemies of the Jews,
to embrace this Jewish man as the Savior? It started with
Jesus asking the woman for a drink of water. He was weary
from walking and hot because it was noon. But Jesus did not
seek to quench His thirst so much as to inflame the spiritual
thirst of the woman.

Christ can refresh us like no drink on earth can. After the
Samaritan woman rather sharply refused Christ's request for

water, He said, "If thou knewest the gift of God, and who it is that saith to thee, Give me to drink; thou wouldest have asked of him, and he would have given thee living water" (John 4:10). "Living water" was an ordinary expression for fresh water (Song 4:15), but Christ implied that He meant something more because He called it "the gift of God." John later explained that this was the gift of the Holy Spirit (John 7:37–39). Christ also prodded the woman to ask who He was to have the power to give her such a divine gift.

Few people see Jesus as the one who can satisfy them. The woman mocked Jesus for His seemingly ridiculous offer of fresh water when He did not even have a bucket. She clearly had her wits about her, though she lacked spiritual insight. She also challenged His promise to give her better water from God, as if He were "greater than our father Jacob, which gave us the well" (John 4:12). Without faith, we see Christ as weak, unable to take care of His own concerns, much less ours. Our very intelligence may blind us to what Jesus offers.

Yet Christ bears patiently with proud sinners and reveals Himself to them. He thus explained to the Samaritan woman that well water satisfies only for a time, but the living water Christ gives is "a well of water springing up into everlasting life" within a person so that he "shall never thirst" (John 4:14). This water springs from an artesian well of supernatural life within the soul. This well is nothing less than the Lord Himself, "the fountain of living waters" (Jer. 2:13; 17:13).

Now we see why Christ said that He alone can satisfy our thirst. First, this living water flows inside our souls. Physical things may please and comfort our bodies, but they cannot satisfy our hearts. Second, the living water is the life of God within the soul. God has made us for Himself, and we will always thirst until we drink deeply of Him.

Many people seek the wrong kind of satisfaction from God. The woman immediately asked Christ for living water, thinking that she would not ever have to draw water from the well again. But Christ gives us a true thirst for Him by convicting us of sin. Thus He invited the woman to call her husband to join them. When she said, "I have no husband," His reply astonished her: "Thou hast well said, I have no husband: for thou hast had five husbands; and he whom thou now hast is not thy husband: in that saidst thou truly" (John 4:17–18). He gently places His finger right on the sore spot of our hearts to show us that we need God.

People don't want to face their thirst. The Samaritan woman thus tried to change the subject by asking Christ who worshiped in the right temple, the Jews or the Samaritans. Jesus said that He was the Christ. Because He has come, God is not concerned with buildings or locations for worship, but with true worshipers who worship the Father in spirit and truth (John 4:19–26). The great age of types and shadows is thus fulfilled in Christ, the living water.

If Jesus Christ has quenched your thirst, His truth will move you to worship God as He commands, calling on the Father, in the name of Christ, and in the power of the Spirit.

TO BE LOVED BY
GOD'S CHILDREN

*Jesus said unto them, If God were your Father, ye would love
me: for I proceeded forth and came from God; neither came I
of myself, but he sent me.*
— JOHN 8:42

Not everyone loves Jesus. We are not referring here to hard-
core pagans and militant atheists but to ordinary religious
people who claim to believe in Jesus but do not love Him at
all. That is what Christ experienced on earth.

The Lord Jesus often offended people by His words
and deeds. Christ once told some people who professed to
believe in Him that only true disciples abide in His Word,
"and ye shall know the truth, and the truth shall make you
free" (John 8:30–32). They objected that they were free
men and the children of Abraham. But Christ told them
they were slaves of sin, and only the Son could set them
free (John 8:33–36). He also said they had rejected His
word and wanted to kill Him because they were children
of the devil, who is a murderer and liar (John 8:37, 43–47).
They responded by telling the Christ of God that He was a
demon-possessed Samaritan!

Belief in Christ and love for Him may evaporate like the
morning dew when He confronts people with their sin and

their need of salvation (John 3:19–20; 15:22–25). As John 6:66 says, "From that time many of his disciples went back, and walked no more with him."

However, Christ did say that the true children of God love Him. He said, "If God were your Father, ye would love me" (John 8:42). Those who love Christ are under God's saving grace (Eph. 6:24). They have not seen Him, but they love Him, trust Him, rejoice in Him, and receive from Him the salvation of their souls (1 Peter 1:8–9). Those who do not love Christ remain under God's curse (1 Cor. 16:22).

The true children of God love His Son as their desire and delight. They love Christ more than they love their parents or their own children (Matt. 10:37). They gladly keep His commandments (John 14:21). They willingly bow before His throne (Ps. 110:1–3). They love Christ more than they love their lives in this world (John 12:25). Why is this so? The Lord Jesus gives us two reasons in John 8:42.

First, they love Him because He comes from the Father. He proceeded from and came from God. The man who walked by the shores of Galilee is the incarnate Son of God, who was with the Father "in the beginning" (John 1:1). He dwells "in the bosom of the Father" (John 1:18) in everlasting, heart-to-heart intimacy with Him (John 17:24). Christ is so closely united to the Father that He could say, "I am in the Father, and the Father in me" (John 14:11). For this reason, whoever has seen the Son has seen the Father (John 14:9).

Every child of God loves Jesus Christ. We see the glory of God shining in the face of Jesus Christ, and our hearts are drawn magnetically to Him (2 Cor. 4:6), for He is our Lord.

The second reason God's children love Christ is because He does His Father's will. All His life on earth was one continuous act of obedience to God. Jesus said, "For I came down from heaven, not to do mine own will, but the will of him that sent me" (John 6:38). Likewise, the heartfelt prayer of every child of God is, "Our Father which art in heaven.... Thy will be done" (Matt. 6:9–10). Whenever they see Christ, the new creation within them thrills with joy because He always does His Father's will, and this joy inclines them to follow in His steps.

Furthermore, they love Christ because the Father sent Him to save sinners. The will of the Father is that His Son bring every person whom the Father chose to eternal life and happiness (John 6:39–40). In the Son, they see how much God loved them when they did not love Him and gave His beloved Son to atone for their sins (1 John 4:9–10).

We love Christ because He first loved us. And the more we see the loveliness of His love, the more we love Him and long to be like Him.

> Grace and truth shall mark the way
> Where the Lord His own will lead,
> If His Word they still obey
> And His testimonies heed.
>
> They that fear and love the Lord
> Shall Jehovah's friendship know;
> He will grace to them accord,
> And His faithful covenant show.
>
> —versification of Psalm 25:10, 14,
> *The Psalter*, no. 65:1, 4

And the Word was made flesh, and dwelt among us, (and we beheld his glory, the glory as of the only begotten of the Father,) full of grace and truth.

—JOHN 1:14

From the dawn of creation, God has been revealing His glory (Ps. 19:1; Rom. 1:20). After man's fall into sin, God spoke to His people through prophets in various times and in different ways (Heb. 1:1). But that was just the glimmering of dawn before the rising of the sun.

The prophets were servants of God, but Jesus Christ is God's Son (Heb. 1:2; 3:5–6). The prophets spoke the word, but Christ is the Word (John 1:1). The prophets were mere moons shining with reflected light, but He is "the Sun of righteousness" (Mal. 4:2), blazing with intrinsic divine radiance (Heb. 1:3). Christ on earth was the supreme revelation of the glory of the triune God.

Many did not see that glory. When Jesus was born, He did not glow in the dark. He had no halo. The signs by which the shepherds identified Him were that He lay in a manger, a feeding trough for animals (Luke 2:12, 16), and was wrapped like any other baby of the time, in swaddling clothes. Those were hardly a crib and raiment fit for a king. Also, when the adult Jesus came to His hometown to teach, the people did not fall at His feet but scorned Him as a hometown kid and son of the local carpenter (Mark 6:3).

The mystery of John 1:14 is that "the Word was made flesh, and dwelt among us." It is truly scandalous to say Jesus was the eternal, personal self-expression of the Father in words such as, "In the beginning was the Word, and the Word was with God, and the Word was God" (John 1:1), meaning that Jesus is the almighty Creator full of life and light (John 1:3–4).

The word *flesh* here refers to human nature in all its lowliness, weakness, and misery since the fall. It is the polar opposite of the divine Word. For as Isaiah 40:6–8 says, "All flesh is grass…. The grass withereth, the flower fadeth: but the word of our God shall stand for ever."

Surely nothing could hide God's glory more than making Him into a suffering, mortal man. If you saw Him gasping in bloody agony upon the cross, you would have thought Jesus scarcely looked human (Isa. 52:14). Is Christ crucified revealing God or hiding Him?

Yet John insists that "the Word was made flesh, and dwelt among us, (and we beheld his glory)." Those who behold His glory see past the externals, for it is a supernatural glory seen only by eyes of faith, enlightened by the Spirit (1 Cor. 2:12). It is a revelation hidden from the wisdom of this world (1 Cor. 2:6–7). Only the Spirit can enable us to see "the glory of God in the face of Jesus Christ" (2 Cor. 4:6).

Christ reveals God's glory, first, in His relationship to the Father: "the glory as of the only begotten of the Father" (John 1:14). No two people were ever closer than the Father and Son (Matt. 11:27). Look at how Christ obeyed His

Father! He hungered to do His Father's will as much as we hunger for our daily food (John 4:34). How deeply delighted the Father was with His Son: "Thou art my beloved Son; in thee I am well pleased" (Luke 3:22)!

Christ reveals God's glory, second, in how He related to people: "full of grace and truth." His divinity sparkled more brightly in His love for sinners than in the greatest miracle He ever performed. That divinity was evident even when Christ was rejected by His own people (John 1:11). Jesus could have come down from heaven like Moses from Sinai with law and thunder to terrify sinners. But Christ revealed God's glory by coming with grace—justifying grace that frees them from their sins, transforming grace that gives them a supernatural new birth, and adopting grace that engrafts them into the family of God (John 1:12–13).

Christ came with grace to prove and confirm the faithfulness of God. He also came full of "truth," the rock-solid fidelity of Israel's covenant Lord, "God, that cannot lie" (Rom. 15:8–9; Titus 1:2). All the promises of God come true in Jesus (2 Cor. 1:19–20). You can trust Him, and in trusting Him you will see God's glorious faithfulness and utter trustworthiness.

NOTES

Preface
1. Charles Spurgeon, *Christ's Incarnation: The Foundation of Christianity* (Pasadena, Tex.: Pilgrim Publications, 1978), 6.

2. John Owen, *Declaration of the Glorious Mysteries of the Person of Christ,* in *The Works of John Owen* (Edinburgh: Banner of Truth Trust, 1976), 1:225.

Chapter 1
1. Andrew Murray, *God's Will* (Springdale, Pa.: Whitaker House, 1982), 37.

2. William Hendriksen, *Exposition of the Gospel of Mark* (Grand Rapids: Baker, 1976), 587.

3. "Form for the Celebration of the Lord's Supper," in *The Psalter* (Grand Rapids: Reformation Heritage Books, 1999), 93.

4. John Calvin, *Calvin's Commentaries* (Grand Rapids: Baker, 1989), Hebrews 10:7.

Chapter 3
1. Calvin, commentary on John 12:47.

Chapter 4
1. *Against Heresies,* 3.18.1, in *Ante-Nicene Fathers,* ed. Alexander Roberts (New York: Scribners, 1903), 446.

Chapter 7
1. "O Jesus, Joy of Loving Hearts," in *Psalter Hymnal* (Grand Rapids: Board of Publications of the Christian Reformed Church, 1976), no. 422.

Chapter 8
1. Augustine, *On the Free Choice of the Will, On Grace and Free Choice, and Other Writings,* ed. Peter King (Cambridge: Cambridge University Press, 2010), 154.

2. Wilhelmus à Brakel, *The Christian's Reasonable Service,* trans. Bartel Elshout, ed. Joel R. Beeke (Grand Rapids: Reformation Heritage Books, 1999), 1:512.

Chapter 9

1. C. S. Lewis, *Mere Christianity* (New York: Harper Collins, 1980), 136–37.

2. Brakel, *Christian's Reasonable Service,* 1:515.

Chapter 10

1. Spurgeon, *Christ's Incarnation,* 28, 34.

2. C. S. Lewis, *The Case for Christianity,* quoted in John Blanchard, *Why on Earth Did Jesus Come?* (Darlington, U.K.: Evangelical Press, 2009), 35.

Chapter 12

1. Calvin, commentary on John 12:50.

Chapter 13

1. Charles Hodge, *Systematic Theology* (Grand Rapids: Eerdmans, 1975), 2:245.

2. John Bunyan, *The Pilgrim's Progress* (Edinburgh: Banner of Truth Trust, 1977), 60.

Chapter 14

1. Brakel, *Christian's Reasonable Service,* 1:513.

Chapter 17

1. Dietrich Bonhoeffer, *The Cost of Discipleship* (New York: Macmillan, 1963), 99.

2. Calvin, commentary on John 12:27.

Chapter 18

1. "I Sought the Lord, and Afterward I Knew," in *Psalter Hymnal,* no. 387.

Chapter 19

1. Hendriksen, *Gospel of Mark,* 414.

Chapter 20

1. Scott MacFarlane *The Hippie Narrative: A Literary Perspective on the Counterculture* (Jefferson, N.C.: McFarland & Co., 2007), 99.

2. Matthew Henry, *Commentary on the Whole Bible,* vol. 6 (McLean, Va.: MacDonald Publishing, n.d.), Ephesians 2:14–22.

Chapter 21

1. J. C. Ryle, *St. Matthew*, in *Expository Thoughts on the Gospels* (New York: Robert Carter & Brothers, 1859), 106.

2. Ryle, *Matthew,* 107.

Chapter 22

1. Alexander Maclaren, *Expositions of Holy Scripture* (Cincinnati: Jennings & Graham, n.d.), Luke 4:21.

Chapter 24

1. Calvin, *Institutes*, 2.12.1.

2. Calvin, *Institutes*, 2.12.2.

3. Calvin, *Institutes,* 2.15.6.

4. Calvin, *Institutes*, 3.3.11.

5. Calvin, *Institutes*, 4.17.9.

6. Dennis E. Tamburello, *Union with Christ: John Calvin and the Mysticism of St. Bernard* (Louisville: Westminster John Knox Press, 1994), 93.

7. Calvin, *Institutes*, 4.17.32.